MANUSCRIPTA

A Journal for Manuscript Research

Volume 63.1
2019

KNIGHTS OF COLUMBUS
VATICAN FILM LIBRARY
SAINT LOUIS UNIVERSITY

BREPOLS

MANUSCRIPTA
A Journal for Manuscript Research

Gregory Pass
Editor

Advisory Board

Jonathan J. G. Alexander
Institute of Fine Arts, New York University

Philip Gavitt
Saint Louis University

Frank T. Coulson
The Ohio State University

Charles H. Parker
Saint Louis University

Albert Derolez
Royal Flemish Academy of Belgium for Sciences and the Artss

Lilian M. C. Randall
Curator of Manuscripts and Rare Books Emerita, The Walters Art Museum

Nancy van Deusen
Claremont Graduate University

Richard H. and Mary A. Rouse
University of California, Los Angeles

Consuelo W. Dutschke
Columbia University

Lucy Freeman Sandler
New York University

A. S. G. Edwards
University of Kent

Barbara A. Shailor
Yale University

Kenneth B. Steinhauser
Saint Louis University

Manuscripta publishes research on the production, dissemination, reception, and transmission of medieval and Renaissance manuscripts, including paleography, codicology, illumination, library history, reading and literacy, textual editing, and manuscript catalogues. Submissions are evaluated through double-blind peer review. Materials for consideration should be sent to vfl@slu.edu, composed in English following the *Chicago Manual of Style* (17th ed.) and using footnote documentation. Provide an abstract of not more than 200 words and ten keywords. See submission guidelines and stylesheet at http://lib.slu.edu/special-collections/publications/manuscripta.

Manuscripta is published twice yearly by Brepols Publishers n.v.
under the auspices of the Knights of Columbus Vatican Film Library, Saint Louis University.
Print and online subscriptions are available through the publisher at
http://www.brepols.net; email periodicals@brepols.net.

© 2019, Brepols Publishers n.v., Turnhout, Belgium. All rights reserved.
No part of this publication may be reproduced, stored in a retrieval system, or transmitted in any form or by any means, electronic, mechanical, photocopying, recording, or otherwise without the prior written permission of the publisher. Printed in the EU on acid-free paper.

D/2019/0095/206
ISBN: 978-2-503-58282-5 / ISSN 0025-2603

CONTENTS

❧

ARTICLES

MATTHEW COLLINS
Copying Illustrations of Dante's *Commedia* from Print to Manuscript: Variations, Ideology, Pedagogy, and Visual Editing • 1–62

BARBARA CROSTINI
Perils of Travel or Joys of Heaven? Reconsidering the Traveling Hypothesis for Bodleian Library, MS E. D. Clarke 15 and the Function of Diminutive Manuscripts • 63–104

TJAMKE SNIJDERS
Behind the Scenes: Establishing a Scriptorium in the Eleventh-Century Monastery of Saint-Sépulcre, Cambrai • 105–145

❧

Index of Manuscripts Cited • 147–151

Copying Illustrations of Dante's *Commedia* from Print to Manuscript: Variations, Ideology, Pedagogy, and Visual Editing

Matthew Collins

It is a well-known practice of illuminators that they would copy directly, or quite closely, from earlier images. Jonathan Alexander has noted that it was a common enough phenomenon for a patron to instruct an artist to derive designs directly from another set of miniatures, as indicated by the very specific language used in the contracts: "secondo modo e forma," in Italian contracts, or "secundum similitudinem et formam," in Latin contracts.[1] In addition to taking their designs from other illustrations,

---

* I would like to thank Lino Pertile, Lilian Armstrong, Arielle Saiber, and Jeffrey Schnapp who read and commented on an earlier version of this article, which has also benefitted from the blind peer review comments.

1. Jonathan J. G. Alexander, *Medieval Illuminators and their Methods of Work* (New Haven, 1992), 53.

Abstract: This study examines how and why illuminators of the late fifteenth and sixteenth centuries copied images from printed book illustrations, focusing upon three manuscripts of Dante's *Commedia* (Paris, Bibliothèque nationale de France, MSS NAF 4530 and 4119; and Florence, Biblioteca Medicea Laurenziana, MS Plut. 40.7) that derived their images from woodcut illustrations of two printed books produced in Venice in 1491. Analysis of the manuscript miniatures and their sources in the printed editions reveal subtle variations indicating particular interests, ideological orientations, and pedagogical concerns of these illuminators.

Keywords: Dante, *Commedia*, Divine Comedy, Illustration, Illumination, Miniatures, Woodcuts, Incunables.

Manuscripta 63.1 (2019) : DOI 10.1484/J.MSS.5.118440

Matthew Collins

or perhaps the drawings upon which they were based, illuminators also commonly used pattern or model books.[2] Within the illustration history of Dante's *Commedia*, a noteworthy case of consistent, systematic copying of a model is clear in London, British Library, Add. MS 19587, a Neapolitan late Trecento manuscript that is directly connected to the mid-Trecento Florence, Biblioteca Medicea Laurenziana, MS Strozzi 152. Millard Meiss believed that "the almost identical compositions ... implies the existence of an earlier Florentine manuscript of this type."[3] Whether there was a shared visual source that has since been lost, or Strozzi 152 was directly observed by the illuminator of Add. 19587, or, to raise a third possibility, the illuminator of Add. 19587 worked from drawings replicating the content of Strozzi 152,[4] the abundant presence of pure (even if occasionally

---

2. For a foundational work on the practice of copying in illuminated manuscripts, see Robert W. Scheller, *Exemplum: Model-Book Drawings and the Practice of Artistic Transmission in the Middle Ages (ca. 900– ca. 1470)* (Amsterdam, 1995), a thorough update of his earlier published *Survey of Medieval Model Books* (Haarlem, 1963). For a recently edited volume consisting of case-studies that bring out the diversity of manners in which model books functioned from the tenth to the fifteenth centuries, see Monika E. Müller, ed., *The Use of Models in Medieval Book Painting* (Cambridge, 2014).

3. Peter Breiger, Millard Meiss, and Charles Singleton, *Illuminated Manuscripts of the Divine Comedy*, 2 vols. (Princeton, 1969), 1:49. Meiss considered several shortcomings (including mere carelessness) in Strozzi 152 as compared to Add. 19587 to be indicative that each was copying, with differing degrees of excellence, what he supposed to be the content of a lost manuscript by Pacino di Bonaguida, which would have been "the first manuscript with illustrations in the lower margins below the text." Yet, the defects he describes could just as easily be the result of a less-than-ideal product of copying from one manuscript to another, perhaps with an intermediary drawing.

4. The third possibility I mention, that a drawing once existed that was used to transmit the designs of Add. 19587 to Strozzi 152, squares well with the fact that the purpose of drawings were essentially regarded during the fourteenth century as being for preparation or transfer. This

Copying Illustrations of Dante's Commedia

imperfect) copying leaves no question that there was some sort of direct influence. The practice of copying among miniaturists of *Commedia* manuscripts also extends beyond the context of books, and of course is true in the case of other illustrated texts as well.[5] For example, as has been well-noted, Nardo di Cione's mid-Trecento fresco in Santa Maria Novella rendering portions of Dante's topographical conception of Hell directly led to the frontispiece of Paris, Bibliothèque nationale de France, MS italien 74, attributed to Bartolomeo di Fruosino.[6]

Another mode of copying by miniaturists, which has been noted beyond the context of *Commedia* illustrations is particular to late fifteenth- and sixteenth-century miniatures: the copying of early printed book illustrations. Rowan Watson, for example, has noted several cases in his study based on the collections of the Victoria and Albert Museum in which the woodcuts of the *Biblia pauperum* printed in Germany in the 1460s were directly copied by a miniaturist in a French book of hours, the so-called Playfair Hours, created roughly two decades later around 1480.[7] Here, I will

---

status explains why it was not until well into the fifteenth century that drawings were preserved in their own right, but leaves open questions of transmission for prior centuries that can never be fully resolved. The possibility of lost drawings derived from Add. 19587 that were used for Strozzi 152 is no less strong than the possibility of a lost archetype from which both sets of miniatures derived.

5. For examples beyond manuscripts of the *Commedia*, a good starting point is Ernst Kitzinger, "The Role of Miniature Paintings in Mural Decoration," in *The Place of Book Illumination in Byzantine Art*, ed. Kurt Weitzmann et al. (Princeton, 1975), 99–142.

6. See Laurence Kanter et al., *Painting and Illumination in Early Renaissance Florence* (New York, 1994), 307–14. For online images, see Gallica, Bibliothèque nationale de France: http://gallica.bnf.fr/ark:/12148/btv1b10500687r?rk=21459;2.

7. London, Victoria and Albert Museum, MS L.475-1918. See Rowan Watson, *Illuminated Manuscripts and their Makers* (London, 2003), 67–68.

Matthew Collins

discuss three illuminated manuscripts of Dante's poem—Paris, Bibliothèque nationale de France, MSS NAF 4119 and 4530; and Florence, Biblioteca Medicea Laurenziana, MS Plut. 40.7—that drew directly from one or both of the illustrated copies of the *Commedia* printed in Venice in 1491 by Bernardinus Benalius and Matteo Capcasa (di Codeca), and by Petrus de Plasiis, Cremonensis.[8] My focus will be to explore the variations found between printed source images and the illuminated renderings produced from them, as well as the ideologies and potential pedagogical aspects they present.[9] Visual editing—by which I mean the active and intentional selection by an artist (and/or advisor) of one or another printed illustration on occasions when more than one image was unquestionably available to the minia-

---

8. Dante Alighieri, *La Commedia*, Venice: Bernardinus Benalius and Matteo Capcasa (di Codeca), 3 March 1491 (ISTC: id00032000); and Dante Alighieri, *La Commedia*, Venice: Petrus de Plasiis, Cremonensis, 18 November 1491 (ISTC: id00033000).

9. There is evidently a revived interest in these later *Commedia* miniatures. In the latest stages of the preparation of this article I learned of two other directly relevant writings that have been published recently, but which I was unable to consult. The first is on the companion manuscripts NAF 4119 and 4530 and their relation to the woodcuts: Gianni Pittiglio "La *Commedia* in chiave trasalpina: Intrecci iconografici tra gli incunaboli veneziani e due codici del *Paradiso* alla corte di Francesco I," *L'Illustrazione: Rivista del libro a stampa illustrato* 2 (2018): 5–20. What he and I write about these manuscripts is in good harmony, even while there are varied emphases and approaches. The most noteworthy variant: he supports an argument that the French miniaturists had Quaregni's 1497 *Commedia*, which reused the woodcuts first printed in Cremonese's November 1491 *Commedia*; I simply refer to the woodcuts as those in the Cremonese printing, where they first appeared. The other work is the recently published facsimile and its commentary volume for Plut. 40.7: Dante Alighieri, *Commedia: Firenze, Biblioteca Medicea Laurenziana, Plut. 40.7; Commentario*, ed. Sonia Chiodo, Teresa De Robertis, Gennaro Ferrante, and Andrea Mazzucchi (Rome, 2018). It will be interesting to see what similarities and differences emerge through these simultaneously conducted studies.

turist(s)—is an important aspect of this process, and is particularly evident in Plut. 40.7.

A fundamental point that emerges from this inquiry is that in late fifteenth- and early sixteenth-century book illustration, artists looked to models when possible, but also made changes in content in response to extant visual sources and other cultural factors, including ideological and pedagogical impulses. It also provides further evidence that images in manuscripts and printed books were understood by artists in this period of technological transition as intrinsically similar and, thus, useful for copying, notwithstanding differences in modes of production and visual media.

PARIS, BIBLIOTHÈQUE NATIONALE DE FRANCE, MSS NAF 4530 AND 4119

These two manuscripts in the Bibliothèque nationale de France are very much companion pieces, each being presentation copies on parchment containing fragments of *Paradiso* as translated by François Bergaigne, who was an otherwise "obscure secretary in princely services" best known for this early French translation of Dante's poem.[10] The first (NAF 4530) is dedicated to Guillaume Gouffier and dated to 1520–25, containing *Paradiso* 1–7, with one miniature per canto; and the second (NAF 4119) is dedicated to Antoine Duprat and dated to 1524–25, containing *Paradiso* 1–11 and 15–20, with six miniatures per canto for cantos 15–20.[11] Blank spaces remain for illuminations to be

---

10. Werner Paul Friederich, *Dante's Fame Abroad, 1350–1850* (Chapel Hill, 1950), 315. See also Richard Cooper, "Praise and (More) Blame of Dante in Late Renaissance Florence," *Yale French Studies* 134 (2018): 67–81.

11. See the dedication in NAF 4530, fol. 2r: "Illustri domino Guiliermo Gouffier, Francie admirato. Franciscus Bergaigne humilem salutem dicit." Duprat is not named in NAF 4119, but his shield appears on fol. 1v, elaborately illuminated and accompanied by two laudatory

added to the earlier cantos in NAF 4119, but captions indicate what they were to be, as indeed do they also for the realized miniatures in both manuscripts.

There can be little doubt that the images of NAF 4530 were taken from one of the Venetian-printed incunables of 1491. Ludwig Volkmann, following Camille Morel, noted that this was the case, though he wrote that "the pictures are copied exactly from the Venetian wood-cuts (no matter which edition),"[12] while Morel stated more observantly that the gestures and arrangements of the figures more precisely align with the woodcuts included in Pietro di Piasi Cremonese's printing dated to November of 1491.[13] Adding to Morel's observation, to which Lamberto Donati also subscribed,[14] an especially immediate distinction between these two very similar woodcuts is in the rendering of the

---

lines of verse. I follow the dating proposed by the Bibliothèque nationale de France for these manuscripts: https://archivesetmanuscrits.bnf.fr/ark:/12148/cc40415n and https://archivesetmanuscrits.bnf.fr/ark:/12148/cc40122m. Minor variations are proposed for these dates, e.g., Arthur Tilley, *The Literature of the French Renaissance* (Cambridge, 1904), 45, suggests a date range of 1517–24 for both manuscripts. Select images only are available for NAF 4530 at Banque d'images, Bibliothèque nationale de France, http://images.bnf.fr/jsp/index.jsp?destination=afficherListeCliches.jsp&origine=rechercherListeCliches.jsp&contexte=resultatRechercheAvancee, while a complete copy of NAF 4119 is available at Gallica, https://gallica.bnf.fr/ark:/12148/btv1b10540048h. For reproductions of both manuscripts, see also Camille Morel, *Les plus anciennes traductions françaises de la Divine comédie publiées pour la première fois d'après les manuscrits*, 2 vols. (Paris, 1895–97).

12. Volkmann, *Iconografia dantesca: The Pictorial Representations to Dante's Divine Comedy* (London, 1899), 89.

13. Morel, *Le plus anciennes traductions*, 2:[3]. The copying is not done quite as "exactement" as Morel claims, but the similarities are nevertheless overwhelming and more than sufficiently definitive.

14. Lamberto Donati, *Il Botticelli e le prime illustrazioni della Divina Commedia* (Florence, 1962), 160–65, generally makes a similar argument regarding the shared presence of a person within the moon in the relevant woodcuts in the November printing and these miniatures, though

moon in the illustrations accompanying *Paradiso* 2–4: those printed by Cremonese (figs. 1–3) include a fleshed out face as well as a fuller, robed figure in canto 2, while those printed by Benali and Capcasa (figs. 4–6) do not. A personified moon is present in the corresponding miniatures of NAF 4530 (figs. 7–9), thus linking them specifically to the Cremonese woodcuts. Since the directly associated companion manuscripts NAF 4530 and 4119 are similar enough that one could argue the same hand illuminated both, which Volkmann indeed does assert,[15] it should come as little surprise that NAF 4119 also specifically used the woodcuts from Cremonese's printing. It should be noted, however, that only the miniatures in NAF 4119 were attributed by Marie-Blanche Cousseau to Etienne Colaud, bearing an implication with which I would agree: namely, that a slightly less skilled artist executed the miniatures in NAF 4530.[16]

We can confirm from minor details distinguishing the two sets of 1491 woodcuts that the Cremonese printing served as the visual source for both NAF 4530 and 4119. Unlike its companion, however, due to the content of the cantos certain apparently insignificant additions by the miniaturist of NAF 4119 not found in the Italian source from which it copied suggests a specific ideological orientation, as we will see. This is not so for every illumination, however, in-

---

he overlooks the further particularly of the figure in *Paradiso* II. Oddly, he does not mention anything regarding NAF 4119.

15. Volkmann, *Iconografia,* 90. Considering the black and white reproductions in Morel's volume that Volkmann relied on, his perception is understandable, as both manuscripts are quite fundamentally similar—not only in following the same woodcut illustrations, but also the additional of architectural framing of the images, and the inclusion of selected captions around which the miniatures are realized. Viewed in color, however, it is immediately evident that the miniatures in NAF 4119 are notably superior to those in NAF 4530.

16. Marie-Blanche Cousseau, *Etienne Colaud et l'éluminure parisienne sous le règne de François 1er.* (Tours, 2016), 171.

Figure 1.

Woodcut illustration for *Par.* 2.
Dante Alighieri. *Comento di Christophoro Landino fiorentino sopra la Comedia di Danthe Alighieri poeta fiorentino.* Impresso in Vinegia: Per Petro Cremonese dito Veronese, [18 November 1491], fol. g v verso (seq. 71). Inc 4482 (21.1).
(By permission of the Houghton Library, Harvard University)

Figure 2.

Woodcut illustration for *Par.* 3.
Dante Alighieri. *Comento di Christophoro Landino fiorentino sopra la Comedia di Danthe Alighieri poeta fiorentino.* Impresso in Vinegia: Per Petro Cremonese dito Veronese, [18 November 1491], fol. g viii recto (seq. 72). Inc 4482 (21.1).
(By permission of the Houghton Library, Harvard University)

Figure 3.

Woodcut illustration for *Par.* 4.
Dante Alighieri. *Comento di Christophoro Landino fiorentino sopra la Comedia di Danthe Alighieri poeta fiorentino*. Impresso in Vinegia: Per Petro Cremonese dito Veronese, [18 November 1491], fol. h ii verso (seq. 73). Inc 4482 (21.1).
(By permission of the Houghton Library, Harvard University)

Figure 4.

Woodcut illustration for *Par.* 2.
Dante Alighieri. *Comento di Christophoro Landino fiorentino sopra la Comedia di Danthe Alighieri poeta fiorentino*. Impressi i[n] Venesia: P[er] Bernardino Benali & Matthio da Parma, [3 March 1491], fol. C iiii verso (seq. 69). Inc 4877 (B) (24.5).
(By permission of the Houghton Library, Harvard University)

Figure 5.

Woodcut illustration for *Par.* 3.
Dante Alighieri. *Comento di Christophoro Landino fiorentino sopra la Comedia di Danthe Alighieri poeta fiorentino.* Impressi i[n] Venesia: P[er] Bernardino Benali & Matthio da Parma, [3 March 1491], fol. C vii recto (seq. 70). Inc 4877 (B) (24.5).
(By permission of the Houghton Library, Harvard University)

Figure 6.

Woodcut illustration for *Par.* 4.
Dante Alighieri. *Comento di Christophoro Landino fiorentino sopra la Comedia di Danthe Alighieri poeta fiorentino.* Impressi i[n] Venesia: P[er] Bernardino Benali & Matthio da Parma, [3 March 1491], fol. D i recto (seq. 71). Inc 4877 (B) (24.5).
(By permission of the Houghton Library, Harvard University)

Figure 7.

Illustration for *Par.* 2.
Paris, Bibliothèque nationale de France, MS NAF 4530, fol. 11v.
(By permission of the Bibliothèque nationale de France)

Figure 8.

Illustration for *Par.* 3.
Paris, Bibliothèque nationale de France, MS NAF 4530, fol. 20v
(By permission of the Bibliothèque nationale de France)

Figure 9.

Illustration for *Par.* 4.
Paris, Bibliothèque nationale de France, MS NAF 4530, fol. 26v.
(By permission of the Bibliothèque nationale de France)

cluding that of *Paradiso* 15 (fig. 10), in which one of two figures to the right side of the image holds a bird; this detail is specific to the woodcuts in the Cremonese printing (fig. 11), and quite distinct from the larger crowd in that of Benali and Capcasa (fig. 12), in which the figure with a bird in hand stands to the left of the kneeling Cacciaguida.[17]

The source for the rendering of *Paradiso* 17 (fig. 13) is also particularly identifiable in the absence of Beatrice behind Dante in the lower register in which Dante kneels before Bartolomeo della Scala; in details potentially indicative of diverging conceptual viewpoints between the 1491 images, the illustration in the Cremonese printing does not include Beatrice (fig. 14), while in the woodcut from the Benali and Capcasa printing she is represented standing behind Dante (fig. 15). Yet again, the miniaturist of NAF 4119 has copied the Cremonese woodcut.

The miniaturist's rendering of *Paradiso* 18 in NAF 4119 (fig. 16) similarly adheres to the corresponding Cremonese woodcut (fig. 17), which is distinct from Benali and Capcasa (fig. 18) in that there are six figures in the lower register, and Cacciaguida as well as the cross formed by heavenly souls are to Dante and Beatrice's right; the upper register is reversed in Benali and Capcasa, and in the lower register of the image there are nine figures, corresponding to all of the "nine worthies" named in lines 37–51 of the canto.[18] In this illumination, we begin to see signs of ideology. Though Co-

---

17. I cannot decipher any literal resonance or expository reason in *Paradiso* 15 for the figure with the bird. The fact, even when the crowds in the lower register were rearranged, that this same bird-bearing individual is still present is all the more curious. The best explanation I can conceive of is that the copyist assumed there was something significant (even if unaware of what that was) in this figure with his bird, and thus, was sure to include this detail.

18. This is an odd visual reading of the text, in that these "nine worthies" in fact are quite specifically those that form the shape of the cross. Neither the woodcut in the Cremonese or the Benali and Capcasa print-

Figure 10.

Illustration for *Par.* 15.
Paris, Bibliothèque nationale de France, MS NAF 4119, fol. 82v.
(By permission of the Bibliothèque nationale de France)

Figure 11.

Woodcut illustration for *Par.* 15.
Dante Alighieri. *Comento di Christophoro Landino fiorentino sopra la Comedia di Danthe Alighieri poeta fiorentino*. Impresso in Vinegia: Per Petro Cremonese dito Veronese, [18 November 1491], fol. l v verso (seq. 84). Inc 4482 (21.1).
(By permission of the Houghton Library, Harvard University)

Figure 12.

Woodcut illustration for *Par.* 15.
Dante Alighieri. *Comento di Christophoro Landino fiorentino sopra la Comedia di Danthe Alighieri poeta fiorentino*. Impressi i[n] Venesia: P[er] Bernardino Benali & Matthio da Parma, [3 March 1491], fol. F viii verso (seq. 82). Inc 4877 (B) (24.5).
(By permission of the Houghton Library, Harvard University)

Figure 13.

Illustration for *Par.* 17.
Paris, Bibliothèque nationale de France, MS NAF 4119, fol. 95r.
(By permission of the Bibliothèque nationale de France)

Figure 14.

Woodcut illustration for *Par.* 17.
Dante Alighieri. *Comento di Christophoro Landino fiorentino sopra la Comedia di Danthe Alighieri poeta fiorentino*. Impresso in Vinegia: Per Petro Cremonese dito Veronese, [18 November 1491], fol. m iii verso (seq. 86). Inc 4482 (21.1).
(By permission of the Houghton Library, Harvard University)

Figure 15.

Woodcut illustration for *Par.* 17.
Dante Alighieri. *Comento di Christophoro Landino fiorentino sopra la Comedia di Danthe Alighieri poeta fiorentino*. Impressi i[n] Venesia: P[er] Bernardino Benali & Matthio da Parma, [3 March 1491], fol. G v verso (seq. 84). Inc 4877 (B) (24.5).
(By permission of the Houghton Library, Harvard University)

Figure 16.

Illustration for *Par.* 18.
Paris, Bibliothèque nationale de France, MS NAF 4119, fol. 101v.
(By permission of the Bibliothèque nationale de France)

Figure 17.

Woodcut illustration for *Par.* 18.
Dante Alighieri. *Comento di Christophoro Landino fiorentino sopra la Comedia di Danthe Alighieri poeta fiorentino*. Impresso in Vinegia: Per Petro Cremonese dito Veronese, [18 November 1491], fol. m vi recto (seq. 87). Inc 4482 (21.1).
(By permission of the Houghton Library, Harvard University)

Figure 18.

Woodcut illustration for *Par.* 18.
Dante Alighieri. *Comento di Christophoro Landino fiorentino sopra la Comedia di Danthe Alighieri poeta fiorentino*. Impressi i[n] Venesia: P[er] Bernardino Benali & Matthio da Parma, [3 March 1491], fol. G vii recto (seq. 85). Inc 4877 (B) (24.5).
(By permission of the Houghton Library, Harvard University)

laud clearly adheres to the Cremonese printing for this rendering as well, he also makes a particularly francophonic addition that indicates he (and/or his advisor) had not simply copied the woodcut thoughtlessly. Rather, he revisited the text, in turn selectively drawing from it to emphasize one particular element: unlike the woodcut from which it directly derived its design, names are inscribed above the head that identify three of the six characters rendered in the lower register. Having evidently accepted that the figures rendered in the Cremonese woodcut and copied in the illumination must be six of Dante's version of the Nine Worthies,[19] Colaud chooses three figures of French history from among the six figures to identify particularly in captioned writing, overlooking characters such as Joshua and Judas Maccabeus: Roland, Charlemagne, and Godfrey of Bouillon, as if they were especially important figures among the nine. We can well suspect the reason for this choice.[20]

---

ings identify this number correctly—rather, the former renders a total of sixteen souls within the form of a cross, and the latter a total of twelve.

19. Dante's version of the Nine Worthies is, of course, quite distinct from the traditional set, which comprises Hector, Alexander the Great, Julius Caesar, Joshua, David, Judas Maccabeus, King Arthur, Charlemagne, and Godfrey of Bouillon. Johan Huizinga attributed the first designation of the traditional nine worthies to Jacques de Longuyon in his *Voeux du Paon* of 1312: see Huizinga, *The Waning of the Middle Ages: A Study of the Forms of Life, Thought and Art in France and the Netherlands in the XIVth and XVth Centuries* (London, 1924), 61.

20. One could argue that this selective identification of personally preferred figures aligns with the spirit of Dante's own maneuver in altering both the order and several of the figures from the traditional list of the Nine Worthies with a strong element of personalization, especially in adding his supposed ancestor Cacciaguida. Roland, as featured in NAF 4119, was another addition by Dante. Best known as a fictional character, above all in the *Chanson de Roland*, his inclusion calls to mind other instances when Dante blurs history and fiction within a theological and/or moral context—for example, in his assertion that Virgil's fictional character of Ripheus is among the blessed in the sphere of Saturn (*Par.* 20.67–72, 118–129). On Dante's familiarity with the traditional Nine Worthies,

Matthew Collins

The next miniature in NAF 4119, representing *Paradiso* 19 (fig. 19), once again follows the particularities of the woodcut in the Cremonese printing (fig. 20), as is most immediately evident in the lower register, in which only a single figure is rendered with sword in hand, chasing another solitary figure, as distinct from the presence of a crowd of soldiers behind the sword-bearing king, and the presence of a flag-bearer accompanying the fleeing figure in the illustration within the Benali and Capcasa woodcut (fig. 21). Like the preceding miniature in this manuscript, another minor addition with a particular ideological bent is made in the form of labelled names, this time with inaccuracies in regard to both the illustrated text and actual historical events. Given that the artist had enough textual familiarity to infer with perfectly understandable reason that the six figures rendered in the illustration of *Paradiso* 18 could represent a selection of the Nine Worthies, and that the artist was also familiar enough to take the opportunity in selectively emphasizing French figures, the presence of erroneous labeling is a bit surprising. The solitary figure bearing a sword is identified in Colaud's image as "Charles," though Dante is referring not to Charles of Anjou, the French-born brother of St. Louis IX, but to his son Charles II, who would hardly have been able to run with sword in hand. Indeed, in this very passage the poet calls him "il Ciotto," *the cripple* (*Par.* 19.127), a very particular identifier of this individual that also confirms he could not be either of the rendered figures. Further, the man fleeing this embodiment of French presence on the Italian peninsula is labelled Frederic, though this is a confusion between the Holy Roman Emperor Frederic II, whose son Manfred had been defeated

---

see Robert Hollander, "Dante and the Martial Epic," *Mediaevalia: A Journal of Medieval Studies* 12 (1989 for 1986): 67–91 at 83–85.

Figure 19.

Illustration for *Par.* 19.
Paris, Bibliothèque nationale de France, MS NAF 4119, fol. 107r.
(By permission of the Bibliothèque nationale de France)

Figure 20.

Woodcut illustration for *Par.* 19.
Dante Alighieri. *Comento di Christophoro Landino fiorentino sopra la Comedia di Danthe Alighieri poeta fiorentino.* Impresso in Vinegia: Per Petro Cremonese dito Veronese, [18 November 1491], fol. n i recto (seq. 88). Inc 4482 (21.1).
(By permission of the Houghton Library, Harvard University)

Figure 21.

Woodcut illustration for *Par.* 19.
Dante Alighieri. *Comento di Christophoro Landino fiorentino sopra la Comedia di Danthe Alighieri poeta fiorentino.* Impressi i[n] Venesia: P[er] Bernardino Benali & Matthio da Parma, [3 March 1491], fol. H i verso (seq. 86). Inc 4877 (B) (24.5).
(By permission of the Houghton Library, Harvard University)

Copying Illustrations of Dante's Commedia

by Charles of Anjou after a long and costly campaign,[21] and Frederick II of Aragon to whom Dante was actually referring in this canto. Aside from textual infidelities—a mere reading of line 127 makes it clear enough that Colaud's assertion through labelling is inaccurate—the historical revision is also quite striking. The Frederic II to whom Dante referred had hardly fled Angevin power. Almost the opposite, in fact: he was the regent and then king of the Kingdom of Sicily, a direct result of the fact that the Angevins had been chased from the island on the infamous day of the so-called Sicilian Vespers, when, according to numerous chroniclers, "death to the French" was the rallying cry in the streets of Palermo.[22] This would have been far from the sort of event that this gesture of selective and inaccurate labelling wished to call to mind.

The final miniature in NAF 4119, representing *Paradiso* 20 (fig. 22), yet again follows the Cremonese woodcuts (fig. 23), though the difference of detail is quite minor. Above all, this difference lies in the placement in the upper register of the illustration of a soul between the grouping of Dante and Beatrice plus the Eagle with which they converse, as rendered in the miniature and the Cremonese woodcut; this soul is located behind Dante and Beatrice in the woodcut

---

21. Jean Dunbabin, *Charles I of Anjou: Power, Kingship and State-Making in Thirteenth-Century Europe* (New York, 1998), 130. Pope Urban IV—a French pope by no coincidence—worked with Charles's brother Louis IX to support Charles's campaign to overthrow Manfred. See letter of Urban IV to Louis IX, 3 May 1264 in *Les registres d'Urbain IV (1261–1264): Recueil des bulles de ce pape publiées ou analysées d'après les manuscrits originaux du Vatican*, ed. Jean Guiraud, 4 vols. (Paris, 1901–58), 2:395–96.

22. Giovanni Villani, *Villani's Chronicle: Being Selections from the First Nine Books of the Croniche Fiorentine*, ed. Philip H. Wicksteed, trans. Rose E. Selfe, 2nd ed. (London, 1906), 267. And as Saba Malaspina recorded it, "Adunatur tumultuosa multitudo dicentium: Moriantur Gallaci, moriantur": *Cronisti e scrittori sincroni della dominazione normanna nel regno di Puglia e Sicilia*, ed. Giuseppe del Re, 2 vols. (Naples, 1845–68), 2:335.

Figure 22.

Illustration for *Par.* 20.
Paris, Bibliothèque nationale de France, MS NAF 4119, fol. 112v.
(By permission of the Bibliothèque nationale de France)

Figure 23.

Woodcut illustration for *Par.* 20.
Dante Alighieri. *Comento di Christophoro Landino fiorentino sopra la Comedia di Danthe Alighieri poeta fiorentino.* Impresso in Vinegia: Per Petro Cremonese dito Veronese, [18 November 1491], fol. n iii verso (seq. 89). Inc 4482 (21.1).
(By permission of the Houghton Library, Harvard University)

Figure 24.

Woodcut illustration for *Par.* 20.
Dante Alighieri. *Comento di Christophoro Landino fiorentino sopra la Comedia di Danthe Alighieri poeta fiorentino.* Impressi i[n] Venesia: P[er] Bernardino Benali & Matthio da Parma, [3 March 1491], fol. H iii verso (seq. 87). Inc 4877 (B) (24.5).
(By permission of the Houghton Library, Harvard University)

accompanying Benali and Capcasa's edition (fig. 24). A possible hint of French pride, though less overt than in the previous two instances, may be manifest once again in labelled names that are not present in the Cremonese woodcut. Here a list of names is presented, this time by the Eagle who addresses Dante, and those chosen by Colaud are Old Testament kings, namely David and Hezekiah. Rather than singling out other named kings in this text with which Italians could more readily identify, such as Trajan and Constantine, those that Colaud has featured are Old Testament figures with whom the French royal linage claimed affiliation, most especially after Louis IX came into the possession of the so-called crown of thorns, leading to an elaborate program of propaganda most notable in the Sainte-Chapelle, which was quite quickly built to house the prized relic. The view was promoted that Christ's crown, now in St. Louis's France, linked the French royal lineage with Christ's consummate role as the offspring of David and, thus, of the Old Testament kings. Claims of a certain mystical transfer of a divinely-charged royal lineage are most notable in the building's stained glass windows. Two things are quite clear in regard to NAF 4119: Colaud used Cremonese's woodcuts in particular, welcoming the design of the image, but was not afraid of subtly changing the content of his source images to convey a more francophonic message.

One might claim that the need to copy woodcut illustrations of the *Commedia* by the later miniaturists of these two sixteenth century French manuscripts could have been due to a lack of familiarity and/or ease with the content of Dante's poem. Such chronological, cultural, and geographical dislocation might explain the need to rely on images already created by artists closer to the origin of the text's language and place of production. Indeed, Volkmann essentially considered this to be a certain cause for the copying in these French manuscripts, writing that "the foreign artist was not very well acquainted with the poem, and was obliged to seek for a model for the subject of his representations."[23] One could support this argument further by adding certain errors noted earlier, most especially the apparent confusion (if not viewed as an intentional alteration) between Charles of Anjou and his son, and between Frederick II, the Holy Roman Emperor, whose family Charles chased out, and the Frederick II whose family seized former Angevin territory. However, a considerable degree of familiarity with this text is suggested by the deceptively simple and accurate, yet selective and ideologically motivated, addition of labels to numerous miniatures that were otherwise direct copies, as shown by the principal interest in French characters among Dante's Nine Worthies. Arguments against the ability of the French miniaturists to grasp Dante's language are moot, since the text in the manuscripts within which these miniatures appear is not in Italian but in Bergaigne French translation. But even if lack of familiarity with the text, even in French translation, is an acceptable explanation, it does not account for the parallel phenomenon of Italian illuminators also copying woodcut illustrations, as in the following case.

FLORENCE, BIBLIOTECA MEDICEA LAURENZIANA, MS PLUT. 40.7

An Italian example that also appears to follow the 1491 woodcuts is Plut. 40.7, a late Trecento manuscript with illuminations of *Inferno* executed shortly after the scribal production of the poem, all carried out by one hand, and the commentary all realized by a second,[24] which also in-

---

23. Volkmann, *Iconografia*, 90.
24. On the dating, Massimo Seriacopi has worked, most recently and vigorously, on this manuscript with particular interest in the commentary—in part a copy of Bambaglioli, in part unique and previously unpublished comments. He maintains the dating of the late Trecento; he also affirms the presence of two hands in total in the textual production, one for the poem, another for the previously overlooked commen-

cludes illuminated renderings of *Purgatorio* and *Paradiso* dated by Breiger and Meiss to the late Quattrocento.[25] As Silvia Scipione notes, 1491 is certainly a *terminus post quem* for the miniatures in the *Purgatorio* and *Paradiso*, given the obvious copying.[26] Akin to the previously discussed French illuminations, renderings of each canto, from the first of *Purgatorio* to the last of *Paradiso*, can be identified as following one or the other set of 1491 woodcuts. However, close observation indicates that, unlike the French manuscripts in which the woodcuts of only one of the 1491 editions were used, both sets unquestionably played an influential role in the images created for Plut. 40.7. Further, at least two different miniaturists worked within the same manuscript on *Purgatorio* and *Paradiso* (and taking into account the much earlier realized illustrations of *Inferno*, there are at least three artistic hands). The aesthetic quality is uneven at best, and almost certainly points toward amateur production, as further discussion will demonstrate. If a subtle ideological message emerges from the French copies of *Commedia* woodcuts, a different story emerges from the images within Plut. 40.7, particularly in the *Paradiso* illuminations. We also find in these later-produced miniatures the involvement of numerous illuminators.

---

tary. A thorough description of Plut. 40.7 is given by Massimo Seriacopi, "Un commento inedito di fine Trecento ai canti 2–5 dell'*Inferno*," *Dante Studies* 117 (1999): 199–244 at 202–5. Although it was only twenty years ago that the commentary in this manuscript was seriously studied, the miniatures—particularly of *Purgatorio* and *Paradiso*—have still yet to receive serious attention to the present. Perhaps this is in part because they are not well executed, but they are nevertheless fascinating. Plut. 40.7 is available online at TECA Digitale, Biblioteca Medicea Laurenziana, http://opac.bml.firenze.sbn.it/Manuscript.htm?Segnatura=Plut.40.7.

25. Breiger, Meiss, and Singleton, *Illuminated Manuscripts*, 1:231.

26. Silvia Scipione, *Visualizzazioni dantesche nei monoscritti laurenziani della* Commedia *(secc. XIV–XVI)* (Florence, 2015), 132.

Copying Illustrations of Dante's Commedia

While the specific sources for the miniatures in Plut. 40.7 for the early cantos of *Purgatorio* are not immediately easy to identify because of the similarity of the corresponding woodcut illustrations in both 1491 editions, it becomes evident by *Purgatorio* 12 that there is an unquestionably significant adherence to the woodcuts in the Benali and Capcasa edition (fig. 25). This is clear, first, in the label that identifies Nimrod. The Cremonese woodcutter (fig. 26) managed to write the figure's entire name on a single line above his head, while the Benali and Capcasa woodcutter apparently ran out of space and thus included the label on two horizontal lines as "NENBR-OT."[27] True to the close adherence to the source image (unless altered by ideology, concept, or lack of precision), the miniaturist of Plut. 40.7 (fig. 27) precisely laid out the letters in two lines, in keeping with the Benali and Capcasa woodcut. Another detail that fixes a Benali and Capcasa image as the model for this part of Plut. 40.7 is found in *Purgatorio* 12 where an angel holds out a sword in the act of sending the proud Lucifer below—the sword in the Cremonese woodcut is held almost ninety degrees backward, while in the Benali and Capcasa image, as also in Plut. 40.7, the sword is held horizontally.

The next instance in which a specific woodcut model can be identified is the miniature illustrating *Purgatorio* 19, where the annotation "PAPA ADRIANO V" appears above the head of the figure donning a tiara (fig. 28). This

---

27. I would imagine that, in this case, it would not so much be the designer but the woodcutter whose label wound up on two lines in the Benali and Capcasa edition, and it was likewise the woodcutter who succeeded in avoiding that in the Cremonese edition—hence, I refer specifically to the *woodcutters* rather than *designers* here. Otherwise, in keeping with Arthur Hind's observation that "the most important agent in the making of a woodcut is, generally speaking, the designer," I would emphasize the designer rather than the woodcutter; see Arthur Hind, *An Introduction to a History of Woodcut, with a Detailed Survey of Work Done in the Fifteenth Century*, 2 vols. (London, 1935), 1:30.

Figure 25.

Woodcut illustration for *Purg.* 12.
Dante Alighieri. *Comento di Christophoro Landino fiorentino sopra la Comedia di Danthe Alighieri poeta fiorentino.* Impressi i[n] Venesia: P[er] Bernardino Benali & Matthio da Parma, [3 March 1491], fol. y iii verso (seq. 46). Inc 4877 (B) (24.5).
(By permission of the Houghton Library, Harvard University)

Figure 26.

Woodcut illustration for *Purg.* 12.
Dante Alighieri. *Comento di Christophoro Landino fiorentino sopra la Comedia di Danthe Alighieri poeta fiorentino.* Impresso in Vinegia: Per Petro Cremonese dito Veronese, [18 November 1491], fol. Z i recto (seq. 48). Inc 4482 (21.1).
(By permission of the Houghton Library, Harvard University)

Figure 27.

Illustration for *Purg.* 12.
Florence, Biblioteca Medicea Laurenziana, MS Plut. 40.7, fol. 101v.
(By permission of the Biblioteca Medicea Laurenziana)

Figure 28.

Illustration for *Purg.* 19.
Florence, Biblioteca Medicea Laurenziana, MS Plut. 40.7, fol. 118r.
(By permission of the Biblioteca Medicea Laurenziana)

figure is present in the Cremonese (fig. 29) as well as the Benali and Capcasa editions (fig. 30), but the text identifying the name of the pope is entirely absent in the Cremonese woodcut. Other details later in the illustrations of this canticle, including alignments with otherwise insignificant divergences of labels in *Purgatorio* 24 and 26, further confirm the consistent use of the Benali and Capcasa woodcuts; this consistency remains until the end of *Purgatorio*. It should be noted, though, that while there can be no question that the miniaturist who rendered *Purgatorio* in this manuscript copied one specific set of the 1491 woodcuts—there is no evidence to the contrary—this amateur artist's ability to copy the intended source accurately was significantly limited.[28] This resulted in consistent and most likely unintentional dissonances between these images and their actual visual source. No conceptual or ideological reasons are evident, as for the French manuscripts, and the fairly primitive nature of these images—even when it comes to the basic ability to consistently color within the lines of the still clearly visible pen outlines—would suggest that artistic limitation best explains these variations from the visual source to the present copy.

The 1491 woodcuts have been recognized as the source for the illustrations for *Purgatorio* and *Paradiso* in Plut. 40.7 on three occasions. Breiger and Meiss wrote that "*Purgatorio* and *Paradiso* are copies of woodcuts in the *Commedia* by Bernardino [Benali] and Matteo [Capcasa] da Parma," and they stated that these were carried out by a single artist

---

28. In regard to the aesthetically unsteady and generally less-than-masterful execution of the miniatures in the latter two canticles of Plut. 40.7, one might highlight the fact that this is a rare early *Commedia* manuscript on paper, a difference of material that could have affected the quality of the illuminations. However, the circumstances of the material support cannot provide a full explanation for these renderings, considering that the earlier illuminations of *Inferno* within this very same manuscript are notably better executed.

Figure 29.

Woodcut illustration for *Purg.* 19.
Dante Alighieri. *Comento di Christophoro Landino fiorentino sopra la Comedia di Danthe Alighieri poeta fiorentino.* Impresso in Vinegia: Per Petro Cremonese dito Veronese, [18 November 1491], fol. b iii (seq. 55). Inc 4482 (21.1).
(By permission of the Houghton Library, Harvard University)

Figure 30.

Woodcut illustration for *Purg.* 19.
Dante Alighieri. *Comento di Christophoro Landino fiorentino sopra la Comedia di Danthe Alighieri poeta fiorentino.* Impressi i[n] Venesia: P[er] Bernardino Benali & Matthio da Parma, [3 March 1491], fol. & iiii verso (seq. 53). Inc 4877 (B) (24.5).
(By permission of the Houghton Library, Harvard University)

whom they deemed an "inept amateur."[29] Like his comment on the illuminations in the French manuscripts, Volkmann does not recognize one set of woodcuts as distinguishable from the other, but in essential harmony with Breiger's and Meiss's sentiment regarding the artistic skills involved, he states that these illustrations were executed "very badly."[30] Unlike the others, Scipione makes no value judgement regarding artistic skill, and implies nothing regarding how many hands were involved in the illustrations of the latter two canticles in the MS Plut. 40.7.[31] It has yet to be observed, however, that some of the illuminations of *Paradiso* in this manuscript, even if less than works of true mastery, are quite evidently by a different artist whose technical skill is still relatively superior to that of the one who rendered *Purgatorio*. The slightly improved color palate of the *Paradiso* illuminations (for whatever underlying reasons) alone suggests the involvement of a new illuminator whose work is distinct from that in *Purgatorio*. The presence of better-executed shading in certain of the renderings of *Paradiso* is further indication that we have a distinct hand involved in some of these images. The artist illustrating *Purgatorio* in this manuscript demonstrated no such abilities. Further, there is significant improvement in the accuracy of the copying. The apparently simple act of copying alone is not as easy as it may seem. For an artist to maintain appropriate proportionality is harder than one might suspect, especially when adapting an image from one book to another with a notably different page layout, which requires skills in design to make the necessary adjustments. Such a shift in layout is evident in the illustrations of *Purgatorio* and *Paradiso* in Plut. 40.7, where the square-framed images of the 1491 woodcuts have been adjusted to occupy rectangu-

---

29. Breiger, Meiss, and Singleton, *Illuminated Manuscripts*, 1:231.
30. Volkmann, *Iconografia*, 89.
31. Scipione, *Visualizzazioni*, 32.

lar space in the bas-des-page. Yet the transition from square to rectangular format was evidently more difficult for the artist designing *Purgatorio* than it was for the artist whose involvement first seems to appear in *Paradiso*, and who perhaps also designed (but did not color) most of the illustrations of this final canticle.

Further indication that another artist became involved in the renderings of *Paradiso* in Plut. 40.7 is a heightened editorial selectivity in the use of both sets of 1491 illustrations as sources in this canticle, as opposed to earlier in the manuscript.[32] While there is no evidence that the creator(s) of the images in *Purgatorio* ever observed woodcuts in another printed illustrated edition than that of Benali and Capcasa, it is clear that the Cremonese woodcuts exercised a newfound influence in the *Paradiso* of this manuscript. The most immediately observable example of this influence is the presence of the same clothed figure within the moon (unique to the Cremonese illustration) in *Paradiso* 2, already discussed in identifying the source for NAF 4530. But while the influence of the Cremonese woodcuts is evident in the rendering of *Paradiso* 2 (fig. 31), the illustrations of cantos 3–5 (figs. 32–34) diverge and instead follow Capcasa and Benali, as shown by the faceless moon illustrating these cantos. It is not only the absence of a personified moon that affirms this source, but also the corresponding use of labels: the illustration for *Paradiso* 4 of Benali and Capcasa correctly locates the city of "PALERMO" upon the landmass that is identified as "IXOLA DE CICILIA," as distinct from the Cremonese woodcut in which Palermo is separated from Sicily by a body of water. Here Plut. 40.7 follows Benali and Capcasa.

---

32. This is inaccurately observed by Meiss and Breiger, as well as Scipione, and overlooked by Volkmann. Scipione also claims, probably following Meiss and Breiger, that the sole source for these images was Benali and Capcasa; see Scipione, *Visualizzazione*, 132.

Figure 31.

Illustration for *Par.* 2.
Florence, Biblioteca Medicea Laurenziana, MS Plut. 40.7, fol. 160v.
(By permission of the Biblioteca Medicea Laurenziana)

Figure 32.

Illustration for *Purg.* 3.
Florence, Biblioteca Medicea Laurenziana, MS Plut. 40.7, fol. 162v.
(By permission of the Biblioteca Medicea Laurenziana)

Figure 33.

Illustration for *Par.* 4.
Florence, Biblioteca Medicea Laurenziana, MS Plut. 40.7, fol. 165r.
(By permission of the Biblioteca Medicea Laurenziana)

Figure 34.

Illustration for *Par.* 5.
Florence, Biblioteca Medicea Laurenziana, MS Plut. 40.7, fol. 167r.
(By permission of the Biblioteca Medicea Laurenziana)

For the illustration of *Paradiso* 2, we have an arguably aesthetic reason that the miniaturist aligned with the Cremonese woodcut that includes a robed figure within the moon; in *Paradiso* 4, for which the other set of woodcuts was chosen, there is an issue of informational accuracy, and the illustrator in Plut. 40.7 made the correct choice in following the Benali and Capcasa woodcut. As we can now be certain that both sets of woodcuts were available for the *Paradiso* illustrations, it begins to appear that the choices between one and the other visual source are not merely arbitrary selections, but the product of thoughtful reflection. The miniatures representing *Paradiso* 5, 6, and 7 all specifically follow the Benali and Capcasa woodcuts, as suggested in each case by minor details akin to others that I have presented. In cantos five and six, these variations are insignificant as it relates to matters of aesthetics or textual accuracy; either of the 1491 woodcuts would be equally valid. The seventh canto, on the other hand, includes a distinction that requires one to make a value judgement regarding one or the other visual reading inherent to these two 1491 woodcut illustrations.

As is typical in the illustrations of *Paradiso* in each of the 1491 woodcuts, both renderings of *Paradiso* 7 are divided into two registers. In the upper register, we see Dante and Beatrice in conversation with heavenly souls surrounded by stars, indicating their place within heavenly realms.[33] In the lower register, scenes are rendered that typically align in various ways with the content of the conversations that take place within the illustrated canto. In *Paradiso* 7 Beatrice references (among other things) Adam's failure (*Par.* 7.25–27),

---

33. The presence of stars—and in when in color, yellow stars surrounded a solid blue sky, is a visual motif one finds commonly not only in illustrated books but also, for example, on the ceilings of churches that serve to imply the connection between these particular buildings and the goings on in the heavens.

Copying Illustrations of Dante's Commedia

"dannando sé, dannò tutta sua prole" (*Par.* 7.27), the expulsion from Eden, when he was "sbandita di paradiso" (*Par.* 7.37b–38a), and she relates this to the directly relevant theological topic of Christ's incarnation and crucifixion (*Par.* 7.34–51). Drawing from this content, both 1491 designers have selected two scenes corresponding to her discourse—in the lower left, Adam and Eve, and in the lower right, the manger scene, invoking the birth and thus incarnation of Christ. There is a difference, however, that requires a familiarity with the intertextual source of Dante the poet's passing reference, in the words of Beatrice, to the damnation resulting from Adam's transgression: in both images, Adam, Eve, Eden, the serpent, and the expulsion from the garden are fleshed out—and most of these specific details are not included in this brief reference to the third chapter of the book of Genesis.

To tease out fully the difference between these two illustrations from which the miniaturist(s) selected, we need to consider the source text from which these fleshed out details derive and the varied approaches each woodcut takes in relation to it. There is, in a sense, an inaccuracy in the Cremonese woodcut (fig. 35): Adam and Eve are in the process of partaking of the fruit from the tree of knowledge, the serpent is in conversation with them, they are covering themselves, and they are outside of the garden. These rendered details, in fact, point to three or four distinct moments in the source text: the serpent tempts them to eat the fruit (Gen. 3:1–5), which they do (Gen. 3:6–7). There is no indication that the serpent had left when they began to eat, so a simultaneous illustration of the serpent and of Adam and Eve eating could accurately represent a single moment. Definitively distinct in temporal sequence, however, is the moment that they realize they are naked and cover themselves (Gen. 3:7), and then, also a distinct moment, their expulsion from the garden (Gen. 3:23). Yet, in the Cremonese woodcut—which mistakenly accompanies *Paradiso* 8 in the volume—they eat with the serpent looking on while covering themselves, and further, they are outside a walled structure labelled as earthly paradise. This representation could simply be read as an intentional collapsing of time, which is a common technique in the visual narrative logic of medieval and early modern images,[34] but which a more literally minded individual could nevertheless consider inaccurate. The Benali and Capcasa woodcut (fig. 36) bears two important distinctions that are more plainly accurate on a temporal level: Adam and Eve are eating the fruit of the tree inside an architectural framework, indicating that they are still within the garden, and they are not yet covering themselves. The Benali and Capcasa version captures the specific moment, rather than collapsing several distinct moments. Perhaps betraying a preference for a more literal temporality in visual narrative, the miniaturist in Plut. 40.7 chose to follow the Benali and Capcasa illustration (fig. 37). But perhaps the different visual narrative temporalities may not have been the issue, as there is also a simpler and more immediately obvious explanation for avoiding the Cremonese woodcut here: it inaccurately suggests this canto takes place in the sphere of Mars, as "MARTE" is written at the top of the image, though *Paradiso* 7 in fact takes place within the sphere of Mercury.

Thus far, only the illustration of *Paradiso* 2 in this manuscript has taken the Cremonese, instead of the Benali and Capcasa, woodcuts as a visual source; the next instance in the manuscript when the miniaturist follows a woodcut from the Cremonese printing is *Paradiso* 9 (figs. 38–39), though the logic underlying the selection of this source

---

34. A basic reference point on approaches to visual narrative is Kurt Weitzmann, *Illustrations in Roll and Codex: A Study of the Origin and Method of Text Illustration* (Princeton, 1970), esp. 12–46. Weitzmann also engages with Wichkoff's discourse on the topic. There is yet more to say, and to refine, in teasing out the relations between textual and visual narrative, especially in medieval and Renaissance literary illustration.

Figure 35.

Woodcut illustration for *Par.* 7 (but accompanying *Par.* 8).
Dante Alighieri. *Comento di Christophoro Landino fiorentino sopra la Comedia di Danthe Alighieri poeta fiorentino*. Impresso in Vinegia: Per Petro Cremonese dito Veronese, [18 November 1491], fol. i v verso (seq. 77). Inc 4482 (21.1).
(By permission of the Houghton Library, Harvard University)

Figure 36.

Woodcut illustration for *Par.* 7.
Dante Alighieri. *Comento di Christophoro Landino fiorentino sopra la Comedia di Danthe Alighieri poeta fiorentino*. Impressi i[n] Venesia: P[er] Bernardino Benali & Matthio da Parma, [3 March 1491], fol. E i recto (seq. 74). Inc 4877 (B) (24.5).
(By permission of the Houghton Library, Harvard University)

Figure 37.

Illustration for *Par.* 7.
Florence, Biblioteca Medicea Laurenziana, MS Plut. 40.7, fol. 172r.
(By permission of the Biblioteca Medicea Laurenziana)

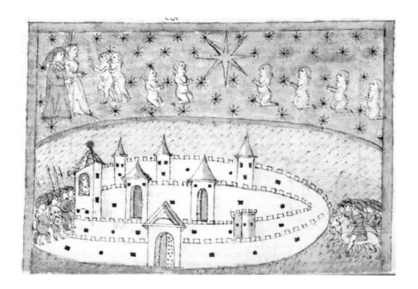

Figure 38.

Illustration for *Par.* 9.
Florence, Biblioteca Medicea Laurenziana, MS Plut. 40.7, fol. 177r.
(By permission of the Biblioteca Medicea Laurenziana)

Figure 39.

Woodcut illustration for *Par.* 9.
Dante Alighieri. *Comento di Christophoro Landino fiorentino sopra la Comedia di Danthe Alighieri poeta fiorentino.* Impressi i[n] Venesia: P[er] Bernardino Benali & Matthio da Parma, [3 March 1491], fol. E v recto (seq. 76). Inc 4877 (B) (24.5).
(By permission of the Houghton Library, Harvard University)

Figure 40.

Woodcut illustration for *Par.* 9.
Dante Alighieri. *Comento di Christophoro Landino fiorentino sopra la Comedia di Danthe Alighieri poeta fiorentino.* Impresso in Vinegia: Per Petro Cremonese dito Veronese, [18 November 1491], fol. i viii recto (seq. 78). Inc 4482 (21.1).
(By permission of the Houghton Library, Harvard University)

is less explicable. The only difference between the illustrations is one of simple labeling, a detail that these miniatures also willingly and precisely copy, as we have already seen. Both illustrate the story of Rahab the Harlot, who aided the Jews in their invasion of Jericho; she is named as present in the sphere of Venus (where Dante the pilgrim is located in this canto), and her redemptive act that is featured here as the scene occupying the lower register in both woodcuts is passingly referenced as the reason for her eternal position: "perch' ella favorò la prima Gloria / di Iosüè in su la Terra Santa" (*Par.* 9.124–125).[35] In the Benali and Capcasa woodcut, "RAB" in inscribed above Rahab's head, and "HIERICO" above the rendered city, both with perfectly good cause; in the Cremonese woodcut (fig. 40) these labels are absent, as they are in the illustration of *Paradiso* 9 in Plut. 40.7. Unlike the previously described reasons for selecting one or the other set of woodcuts, this second instance for choosing the Cremonese illustration in particular has less evident cause.

Sandwiched between images drawn from the Cremonese woodcuts in *Paradiso* 9 (just discussed) and 11 (to be discussed subsequently), for the rendering of *Paradiso* 10 the artist of Plut. 40.7 (fig. 41) draws from the Benali and Capcasa woodcut (fig. 42). Here there is a thorough divergence between these printed illustrations in the lower register, even more clearly forcing a value judgement than, for example, in the illustrations of *Paradiso* 7 with the differing approaches to visualizing the passage of narrative time in the intertext of Genesis 3. In both illustrations, the upper register is the same. In the lower register, Dante and

---

35. "Because she aided Joshua when he gained / his first triumph in the Holy Land" (all translations are from Robert and Jean Hollander, trans., *Paradiso* [New York, 2007]). The source text to which Dante refers, and from which details for the images in the lower registers of both 1491 woodcuts must have derived, is the second chapter in the book of Joshua.

Figure 41.

Illustration for *Par.* 10.
Florence, Biblioteca Medicea Laurenziana, MS Plut. 40.7, fol. 179v.
(By permission of the Biblioteca Medicea Laurenziana)

Figure 42.

Woodcut illustration for *Par.* 10.
Dante Alighieri. *Comento di Christophoro Landino fiorentino sopra la Comedia di Danthe Alighieri poeta fiorentino.* Impressi i[n] Venesia: P[er] Bernardino Benali & Matthio da Parma, [3 March 1491], fol. E vii recto (seq. 77). Inc 4877 (B) (24.5).
(By permission of the Houghton Library, Harvard University)

Beatrice are rendered in conversation with Thomas Aquinas in the Cremonese woodcut (fig. 43). This is inconsistent with the tendency among these illustrations of *Paradiso* to represent an element of the content of a conversation on the lower register, leaving the representation of the conversing figures to the upper register. More confusing, though, is what is in the lower register in the Benali and Capcasa woodcut: a representation of Phaeton, as the label above the head of the central figure makes explicit, who is rendered immediately after he has plunged and is now sinking into the River Eridanus, surrounded by his sisters who are in the midst of their transformation into trees.[36] Explicitly named twice in the *Commedia* (*Inf.* 17.125 and *Par.* 31.124), Phaeton is neither named nor indirectly referenced in *Paradiso* 10. This could be one of the fairly unusual cases of a strong visual reading by one among the illustrators of the early printed editions of the poem, a general topic best left for another occasion, though present circumstances call for a hypothesis here regarding this particular image.

A point Kevin Brownlee made in his study on direct and implied references to Phaeton in the *Commedia* could perhaps shed light on this curious choice. Responding particularly to the reference to Phaeton in the context of Geryon's descent while suggesting broader implications, Brownlee writes that "an almost symmetrical inversion of Phaeton's experience is being effected by Dante the protagonist,"[37] and he goes on to refer to Dante as a "'corrected' Phaeton."[38] It is somewhat understandable, if the artist (and/or advi-

---

36. All of these details correspond perfectly well to Ovid's recounting of the tale in *Metamorphosis* 1.748–79 and 2.1–406, except that Phaeton has three sisters, not six—perhaps three more figures are added in this illustration simply to fill in space. Also, Phaeton's sisters do not attempt to pull him from the river, as they are attempting to do in the image.

37. Kevin Brownlee, "Phaeton's Fall and Dante's Ascent," *Dante Studies* 102 (1984): 135–44 at 137.

38. Ibid., 138.

Figure 43.

Woodcut illustration for *Par.* 10.
Dante Alighieri. *Comento di Christophoro Landino fiorentino sopra la Comedia di Danthe Alighieri poeta fiorentino*. Impresso in Vinegia: Per Petro Cremonese dito Veronese, [18 November 1491], fol. k ii verso (seq. 79). Inc 4482 (21.1).
(By permission of the Houghton Library, Harvard University)

Figure 44.

Woodcut illustration for *Par.* 11.
Dante Alighieri. *Comento di Christophoro Landino fiorentino sopra la Comedia di Danthe Alighieri poeta fiorentino*. Impressi i[n] Venesia: P[er] Bernardino Benali & Matthio da Parma, [3 March 1491], fol. F iiii verso (seq. 80). Inc 4877 (B) (24.5).
(By permission of the Houghton Library, Harvard University)

sor) were aware of and desirous to draw this contrast between Dante and Phaeton, that the sphere of the sun could be seen as an opportune moment to do so. This is especially so given that the pattern of design in the *Paradiso* illustrations lends itself to the representation of narratives sometimes only passingly referenced in the corresponding canto. In this case, there is no direct connection, even implied, to the story in the content of this canto. Nevertheless, there is the appearance of a continuation of the pattern in these *Paradiso* illustrations, and again, the sphere of the sun does lend itself to drawing out the contrast between Dante the pilgrim and Phaeton: while we see the pilgrim rendered upon his arrival in the upper register at the sphere of the sun, which Phaeton unsuccessfully attempted to steer, Phaeton is shown in the lower register in his demise as a direct antithesis to the ascending pilgrim, somewhat reminiscent of the manner in which Dante's Ulysses and his "folle volo" ("mad flight," *Inf.* 26.125) contrasts with Dante, the pilgrim and the poet.[39] Ultimately, we cannot truly conclude why the designer of this particular illustration chose to include the story of Phaeton in the lower register—if there is any interpretively intentional reason at all—but, in an action no less curious than the first artist's decision, the miniaturist rendering *Paradiso* 10 in Plut. 40.7 chose to follow this version of the two visual approaches to the canto in the 1491 woodcuts.

We are in no better position to determine why this image was chosen from between these two actively used sources by the miniaturists than we are to conclude the actual reason that Phaeton is present in the Benali and Capcasa woodcut, but the possibilities that seem most likely are as follows: the

---

39. On the contrast between Ulysses and Dante, see John Freccero, "Shipwreck in the Prologue," in Freccero, *In Dante's Wake: Reading from Medieval to Modern in the Augustinian Tradition,* ed. Melissa Swain and Danielle Callegari (New York, 2015), 1–18.

rendering of a story in the lower register, rather than the figures in conversation within the canto, better fits the pattern of the *Paradiso* illustrations; or, the image was simply considered more visually compelling and dynamic for reasons completely unrelated to its referential or conceptual content; or, the miniaturist reflected on the potential implications and rather liked the strong visual reading involving Phaeton. Whatever the case, it was the Benali and Capcasa woodcut that was chosen for Plut. 40.7, even while the Cremonese woodcuts were used as visual sources for the illustration of the preceding canto and for the one that followed.

Divergences between the two 1491 illustrations of *Paradiso* 11 again call for a value judgement. In the upper register of the Benali and Capcasa woodcut (fig. 44), we have a reference to encircling souls in the sphere of the sun, while the Cremonese woodcut (fig. 45) features the focal point of the canto: St. Francis, at the center, to whom St. Thomas is pointing—no doubt referring to the fact that Thomas is the one who tells the tale of Francis's life. Both are perfectly reasonable approaches, as are the differences in the lower register of each woodcut. The scene in the Benali and Capcasa woodcut relates to an earlier moment in Francis' life, briefly referenced in the canto; "giovinetto, in guerra / del padre ... e dinazi a la sua spiritual corte" (*Par.* 11.58b–59a, 61).[40] As recounted in both St. Bonaventure's and Thomas of Celano's lives of St. Francis, to which Dante was no doubt referring, shortly after his conversion Francis was pursued by his father and brought before the bishop of Assisi. This looks to be a reference to that moment, though a saliently missing detail which the visual retelling attributed to Giotto at Assisi (for example) does not overlook is Francis's disrobing. On the right, four men hold books, toward which two are gesturing. A bit hard to decipher, the most likely explana-

---

40. "Still a youth, he fought against his father's wish ... and before his spiritual court."

Figure 45.

Woodcut illustration for *Par.* 11.
Dante Alighieri. *Comento di Christophoro Landino fiorentino sopra la Comedia di Danthe Alighieri poeta fiorentino.* Impresso in Vinegia: Per Petro Cremonese dito Veronese, [18 November 1491], fol. k v recto (seq. 80). Inc 4482 (21.1).
(By permission of the Houghton Library, Harvard University)

Figure 46.

Illustration for *Par.* 11.
Florence, Biblioteca Medicea Laurenziana, MS Plut. 40.7, fol. 182r.
(By permission of the Biblioteca Medicea Laurenziana)

tion for these details is that they reference the explicit reason Francis's father brought him before the bishop: he "was fain to take [Francis], now stripped of his wealth, before the bishop of the city, that into his hands he might resign his claim unto his father's inheritance."[41] In the lower left is a still-robed Francis who gestures toward himself, surrounded by three others including (most likely) his mother whose support was emphasized in the recountings of this episode.

The Cremonese illustration chose for its lower register a later moment in Francis's life, which Dante recounts thoroughly enough in *Paradiso* 11 that it does not require a return to an intertextual source beyond the *Commedia* to flesh out visual details. Standing before a pope (identifiable by the tiara), Francis is in his Franciscan robe and surrounded by fellow friars who are similarly dressed. This is probably not his appearance before Pope Innocent III, from whom he received the "primo sigillo a sua religïone" (*Par.* 11.93),[42] as this scene with Franciscan friars would seem to indicate an already-founded order.[43] It seems more likely that it is Francis's appearance before another pope, Onorius III, when he received a "seconda corona" (*Par.* 11.97).[44] The Cremonese scene is less idiosyncratic and more immediately recognizable than the Benali and Capcasa illustration in the lower register, with less confusing details. As such, it is understandable why the miniaturist would choose to follow the Cremonese woodcut—though adding an even greater number of Franciscans in the lower register (fig. 46), which may only further emphasize the fact that the order was already quite influential, perhaps thereby lending greater certainty

---

41. St. Bonaventure, *The Life of St. Francis*, trans. E. Gurney Salter (London, 1904), 17.
42. "The first seal of his order."
43. I cannot say this with full assurance because in the Upper Church of San Francesco at Assisi the fresco cycle attributed to Giotto Francis is already surrounded by robed friars in his encounter with Innocent III.
44. "Second crown."

as to which of the papal visits is rendered here. Even if either image would be a perfectly acceptable choice, the Cremonese illustration does seem to be the stronger of the two.

As I have indicated earlier, the quality of illustration in the second and third canticles of Plut. 40.7 varies considerably, being executed by at least two, possibly more, hands. The illustrations of *Purgatorio* consistently show a low level of skill, while those of *Paradiso* possess an improved color palette, some evident facility with shading, and greater accuracy in copying—not all, however, present simultaneously, with the exception of illustrations in the first two cantos (figs. 47 and 31). Altogether, they exhibit an amateur aspect.[45] One could argue that the same artist had simply improved, returning to *Paradiso* after further learning and practice. The fact that the Cremonese woodcuts were taken into account in this third canticle may well point to a gap in time, when this other set of 1491 printed illustrations became available to the artist(s) creating designs in this manuscript. But in addition to aesthetic improvements, there is something else striking in these opening illuminations: a third image that seems to be carried out entirely by the same hand (fig. 48), which is the only instance among all the miniatures in the latter two canticles in Plut. 40.7 that does not explicitly and fully copy one or the other of the 1491 woodcuts.[46]

The second illustration of *Paradiso* 1 marks the moment at which Dante and Beatrice transition into the first of the heavenly spheres: "Beatrice tutta ne l'etterne rote / Fissa con li occhi stave; e io in lei / E le luci fissi, di là sù

---

45. Alexander, *Medieval Illuminators*, 178, notes that "a history of the amateur artist needs to be written," which remains so.

46. I say *fully* because the rendering of Beatrice, surrounded by rays of light, and Dante beside her is similar to the way they are rendered in Benali and Capcasa's *Paradiso* 1 woodcut. The image as a whole, however, has not full source in the woodcuts, on in this detail.

Figure 47.

Illustration for *Par.* 1.
Florence, Biblioteca Medicea Laurenziana, MS Plut. 40.7, fol. 158r.
(By permission of the Biblioteca Medicea Laurenziana)

Figure 48.

Illustration for *Par.* 1.
Florence, Biblioteca Medicea Laurenziana, MS Plut. 40.7, fol. 159r.
(By permission of the Biblioteca Medicea Laurenziana)

rimote" (*Par.* 1.64–66).[47] In this miniature Dante looks at Beatrice who in turn looks and gestures toward a literally rendered (though in the text, metaphorical) wheel of the eternal celestial spheres.[48] Though a simple scene in terms of design, in uniquely selecting this passage for an original image, the miniaturist identified an especially pivotal moment in *Paradiso*, the beginnings (and cause) of Dante's ever-increasing experience of what it is to *trasumanar* (*Par.* 1.70).[49] This textually-reflective illustration may well be understood in relation to the aforementioned visual editing practices through *Paradiso* 11, in selecting between one or the other of the 1491 woodcuts, in that both suggest a well-grounded understanding of the text being illustrated. But none of this yet precludes the possibility that the same artist who did the *Purgatorio* illustrations has now returned with improved skills, and perhaps even an increased desire to reflect upon the relations between the text and these illustrations to the point that this artist was even inspired to create a newly designed image. More definitive evidence that additional hands were involved in the creation of these miniatures emerges by reflecting on the images which follow these initial illustrations of the opening cantos of *Paradiso*.

In *Paradiso* 4 (fig. 33) we begin to see the colorist's inability, at times, to stay within the lines as is often the case in the illustrations of *Purgatorio*, and the garments—except for Beatrice's—are no longer treated with any shading, but are once again reduced to a single blob of color, as was also

---

47. "Beatrice had fixed her eyes/ upon the eternal wheels and I now fixed / my sight on her, withdrawing it from above."

48. A similar strategy of literalizing metaphors and similes is taken by Giovanni di Paolo in his illuminations of *Paradiso* in London, British Library, Yates-Thompson MS 36. See John Pope-Hennessy, *Paradiso: The Illuminations to Dante's Divine Comedy by Giovanni di Paolo* (New York, 1993).

49. *Trasumanar* is a neologism, which the Hollanders agreeably translate as: "to soar beyond the human."

previously the case in the *Purgatorio* illustrations. The same is true for the renderings of the fifth and sixth cantos (figs. 34 and 49). In addition to the fact that Beatrice's clothing is uniquely well-rendered in several images in a row now, another particular detail in the illustration of *Paradiso* 6 begins to suggest that two hands may be at work within the same image: the architectonic features that operate as visual shorthand for the city of Rome on the lower right part of the image are quite skillfully shaded; it is difficult to imagine that the artist who worked on this portion of the miniature was the same person who colored in Dante's clothing in this illustration. With very few exceptions (in *Paradiso* 4, for example, the shading is incomplete), architectural features in the illustrations of *Paradiso* in this manuscript are consistently rendered with this same level of skill,[50] even when the rest of a given miniature is evidently the work of someone with lesser abilities.

The decrease in artistic quality, specifically related to coloring, becomes further evident by the illustration of *Paradiso* 11 (fig. 46): with the exception of Beatrice's garment, for which there is still some attention to shading, almost the entirety of the image is inferior to the two illustrations of *Paradiso* 1 (figs. 47–48) and the rendering that accompanied the second canto in this manuscript (fig. 31). An even lesser quality emerges, for which the illustration of *Paradiso* 21 is especially telling (fig. 50), which likely indicates that in the illustrations of *Paradiso* in Plut. 40.7, perhaps two or three individuals participated with lack in skill to varying degrees as compared to the hand involved in the creation of the first three illustrations of the third canticle.

The underlying design—which is to say, materially speaking, the sketches in pen that remain very evident—

---

50. This is the case for the renderings of *Paradiso* 3 (fol. 162v), 6 (fol. 169r), 7 (fol. 172r), 8 (fol. 174r), 16 (fol. 194v), 17 (fol. 197r), 23 (fol. 212r), and 31 (fol. 232v).

Figure 49.

Illustration for *Par.* 6.
Florence, Biblioteca Medicea Laurenziana, MS Plut. 40.7, fol. 169r.
(By permission of the Biblioteca Medicea Laurenziana)

Figure 50.

Illustration for *Par.* 21.
Florence, Biblioteca Medicea Laurenziana, MS Plut. 40.7, fol. 207r.
(By permission of the Biblioteca Medicea Laurenziana)

is almost always of better quality than that which one finds in the renderings of *Purgatorio* in Plut. 40.7. While the coloring of *Paradiso* varies in its degree of evident skill, sometimes varying even within the same miniature, the copying of fundamental design varies far less. There are several images that fall notably short, such as the poorly-spaced copy of *Paradiso* 9 (fig. 38), but it is an exception to otherwise marked improvements as compared to the miniatures of the previous canticle. An especially striking case which reaffirms a difference in skill of the designer (and perhaps sometimes colorist) between most of the *Paradiso* images and those of *Purgatorio* in this manuscript is the manner in which *Paradiso* 29 (fig. 51) is more freely borrowed, even while the coloring is less than outstanding; given the chaotic nature of the illustrations of this canto in both of the 1491 woodcuts (fig. 52), this artist, perhaps recognizing personal limitations and/or the coloring limitations of the others involved, significantly reduced the complexity of the image—but in a fashion that conveys, in its own right, a certain dynamism which points to a recognizable level of relative artistic acumen.

What might be the story behind these curious illustrations of *Purgatorio* and *Paradiso*? In part, Seriacopi's passing observation of these images, after a more serious meditation on those of *Inferno*, may be correct: they are "più ingenui disegni con intenti didascalici che vere e proprie miniature."[51] Rhetorically I would disagree with imbuing the word *miniature* with implications of a certain level of technical ability, and a closer look suggests that some details in the illustrations of this third canticle are not entirely naïve. But I agree that they do seem to betray certain didactic intentions—especially the miniatures accompanying *Paradiso*, in which at least one or more less-skilled

---

51. Seriacopi, "Un commento," 205 ("more naïve, with didactic intentions, than true and proper miniatures").

Figure 51.

Illustration for *Par.* 29.
Florence, Biblioteca Medicea Laurenziana, MS Plut. 40.7, fol. 227r.
(By permission of the Biblioteca Medicea Laurenziana)

Figure 52.

Woodcut illustration for *Par.* 29.
Dante Alighieri. *Comento di Christophoro Landino fiorentino sopra la Comedia di Danthe Alighieri poeta fiorentino.* Impressi i[n] Venesia: P[er] Bernardino Benali & Matthio da Parma, [3 March 1491], fol. K iii verso (seq. 96). Inc 4877 (B) (24.5).
(By permission of the Houghton Library, Harvard University)

image-makers appear to have worked alongside a relatively better-skilled artist, as if in a mock workshop of amateurs. Seriacopi elsewhere argued that this manuscript was owned by the Delfini of Venice,[52] which could better explain the evident access to not only one but both illustrated editions of 1491 printed in that city. One could imagine (but admittedly not prove) that young men and women of this family worked together with a more skilled and learned elder family member or tutor. Because of Dante's status as *auctor* by the end of the Trecento,[53] his *Commedia* was used for pedagogical purposes during this time.[54] Further, students did add illustrations to their schoolbooks, and in several cases, illuminated manuscripts were copied by students in their books.[55] Perhaps the copies in the MS Plut. 40.7 were part of a process of learning to color images, but considering the added element of visual editorial choices, it may well have also been an exercise of learning the content of the text by extensively and actively engaging with its visual representation. This would align well with other indications that the early printed *Commedia* illustrations, being copied here in Plut. 40.7, were incorporated into practices of reading, including pedagogical and mnemonic undertakings.[56]

---

52. Massimo Seriacopi, "Il canto III dell'Inferno in un comment inedito di fine Trecento," *Tenzone* (2001): 221–26 at 221–22.

53. On the emergence of the medieval *auctor*, see Alastair Minnis, *Medieval Theory of Authorship: Scholastic Literary Attitudes in the Later Middle Ages*, 2nd ed. (Philadelphia, 2010), and on Dante's place within these major changes in the concept of authorship, see Albert Ascoli, *Dante and the Making of the Modern Author* (Cambridge, 2008).

54. Robert Black, *Education and Society in Florentine Tuscany: Teachers, Pupils and Schools, c.1250–1500* (Leiden, 2007), 81.

55. Robert Black, *Humanism and Education in Medieval and Renaissance Italy: Tradition and Innovation in Latin Schools from the Twelfth to the Fifteenth Century* (Cambridge, 2001), 312–13.

56. There is much yet to be said about the connections between mnemonics, Dante's work, and the illustrations of Dante's work. The mnemonic quality of Dante's *Commedia* was noted by Francis Yates, *The Art*

CONCLUSION

62 In addition to demonstrating the porous relationship that existed between early printed books and manuscripts—here in regard to images in each form of book production—another broader point emerges from this study. For various reasons, artists also made active, intentional decisions that resulted in changes between the source image and its copy. Sometimes these changes were apparently insignificant, yet revealing; for example, the choice of adding name labels for certain rendered figures, revealing a pattern of subtle propaganda. Within the limited context of the three manuscripts studied here illustrating the *Commedia*, a variety of motivations affected the rationale for visual edits, including ideology, pedagogy, aesthetics, as well as textual and factual fidelity. When it comes to medieval and Renaissance literary illustration, even questions of visual genealogies developed through copying—which may seem to belong more to the realm of image making—are fascinatingly complicated by evident reconsiderations rooted in details within the literary work being illustrated, or in the other considerations that were informed by specific cultural contexts.

Harvard University

---

of Memory (Chicago, 1966), 95, who observed that "Dante's *Inferno* could be regarded as a kind of memory system." The most sustained attention dedicated to the question of Dante mnemonics is Spencer Pearce, "Dante and the Art of Memory," *The Italianist* 16 (1996): 20–61. Specifically related to *Commedia* illuminations, Paul Papillo, "Rogue Images in Manuscripts of the Divine Comedy," *Word & Image* 23 (2007): 421–38 at 421, has suggested that the late Trecento illuminated *Commedia*—New York, Morgan Library and Museum, MS M.676—may have borne a mnemonic function.

Perils of Travel or Joys of Heaven? Reconsidering the Traveling Hypothesis for Bodleian Library, MS E. D. Clarke 15 and the Function of Diminutive Manuscripts

Barbara Crostini

Portability as a key factor in the success of the codex form of the book has been part of the discussion of this technological innovation in Late Antiquity from the outset.[1] Michael McCormick has stressed that the itinerant activities of the likely first users of bound parchment codices, such as doctors, teachers, and Christian missionaries, necessarily found the easier accessibility of information in the codex format superior to the clumsy and messy han-

---

1. Notwithstanding recent refinements, the *locus classicus* for this discussion remains Colin H. Roberts and Theodore C. Skeat, *The Birth of the Codex* (Oxford, 1983).

Abstract: This paper examines the function and purpose of small format Byzantine Greek psalters. It addresses specifically Marc Lauxtermann's proposal that, on the basis of its small size, Oxford, Bodleian Library, MS E. D. Clarke 15 was made for the purpose of travel. Contrary to Lauxtermann's literal reading of travel metaphors in the poems of the book's owner, Mark the Monk, I argue that size and portability are not reliable indicators of a travel function. Instead, by interpreting these travel metaphors as indicative of spiritual conversion and placing Clarke 15 within the context of Annemarie Weyl Carr's category of "diminutive manuscripts," I show that this manuscript and other such small psalters were produced as gifts to mark the entry into monastic life of the individual making profession.

Keywords: Psalters, Greek Manuscripts, Byzantine Manuscripts, Travel, Poetry, Monastic Profession.

dling of rolls and scrolls.² Qualities such as compactness, durability, and easy reference were clearly advantages in the practical use of books. Codices could contain a lot of text and were easy to pack and to read from.

The advantage of portability to the owners of books is clear from many different signs. Manuscripts did travel, as Peter Schreiner has shown with a few unequivocal examples of long-distance displacement,³ movements that Irmgard Hutter had already begun to outline through her detailed study of notes in codices.⁴ Records for such displacements were in these cases securely identified from place annotations found within the manuscripts themselves, which allow their itineraries to be traced with precision. From this body of evidence, comprising both small and large codices, it would appear that size was not a determining factor. For example, the large book, Vienna, Österreichische Nationalbibliothek, MS suppl. gr. 47, measuring 280 x 220 mm. and containing 100 folios, was taken on a long a journey.⁵ If the Codex Sinaiticus was ever made for reaching a destination different from its place of production, such a journey would have been secured on a donkey cart, or aboard a ship, probably within a wooden chest not easily lifted by the fainthearted.⁶ The Bible, of all texts *the* one to which Christians would want ready access, was too bulky in

---

2. Michael McCormick, "The Birth of the Codex and the Apostolic Life-Style," *Scriptorium* 39 (1985): 150–58; see also Harry Y. Gamble, *Books and Readers in the Early Church: A History of Early Christian Texts* (New Haven, 1995).

3. Peter Schreiner, "Handschriften auf Reisen," *Bollettino della Badia greca di Grottaferrata* 51 (1997): 145–65.

4. Irmgard Hutter, *Corpus der byzantinischen Miniaturenshandschriften*, 5 vols. (Stuttgart, 1977–97), 4.1:xxix–xxxi. The travels here described are more discreet changes of ownership than actual displacements.

5. See Schreiner, "Handschriften," 158 and n46, 159 map 4 and fig. 6.

6. Theodore Skeat, "Sinaiticus, Vaticanus, and Constantine," *Journal of Theological Studies* 50 (1999): 583–625, esp. 605–9. Codex Sinaiticus is now available online: http://www.codexsinaiticus.org.

Perils of Travel

Late Antiquity to make good travel reading. None of the examples of books that actually travelled would have required special accommodation. However, manuscripts that did travel were not necessarily manuscripts purposefully made for traveling.

Large, single volume pandect bibles soon faded out of fashion, it seems.[7] They were never intended for portability and certainly were not convenient to read. Single texts, and among them especially the New Testament and the Psalms, were more easily copied, read, and widely circulated. It is therefore tempting to deduce that some of the surviving examples, especially those coming in smaller formats, were intentionally made for travel. Precisely this suggestion has been advanced by Marc Lauxtermann for an eleventh-century psalter: Oxford, Bodleian Library, MS E. D. Clarke 15.[8] It is worth reflecting on whether size as a factor self-evidently makes a small manuscript a product designed for traveling. This area of study has been usefully mapped out in a seminal article by Annmarie Weyl Carr on diminutive manuscripts, as she pointedly styled them,[9] which will inform my discussion. Weyl Carr's keen observations on the approaches to understanding the production of such objects in Byzantium continue to be valuable. To anticipate my conclusions about our ability to identify what Greek manuscripts could have been made specifically for travel purposes, I am generally skeptical, particularly

---

7. Skeat, "Sinaiticus," 616–17, makes the point that they were at all times the exception.

8. Marc Lauxtermann, "The Perils of Travel: Mark the Monk and Bodl. E. D. Clarke 15," in *Poetry and its Contexts in Eleventh-Century Byzantium*, ed. Bernard Floris and Kristoffel Demoen (Farnham, UK, 2012), 195–206.

9. Annemarie Weyl Carr, "Diminutive Byzantine Manuscripts," *Codices manuscripti* 6 (1980): 130–61, repr. in Weyl Carr, *Cyprus and the Devotional Arts of Byzantium in the Era of the Crusades* (Aldershot, UK, 2005), no. V.

so in the case of Clarke 15. In contemplating some of these diminutive books, I will tentatively suggest an alternative context for the production of very small psalters that specifically applies to the second half of the eleventh century. I will suggest instead that these books were produced as gifts for the occasion of the profession of monastic vows, entering the monastery together with the new member of the community.

LAUXTERMANN'S TRAVELING HYPOTHESIS: A QUESTION OF SIZE

Lauxtermann confidently affirms that Clarke 15 was made to accompany its owner, Mark, on a perilous journey. He constructs his argument by intertwining the interpretation of the poetic texts specifically made for this codex and observations concerning its size. In his opening sentence, Lauxtermann describes Clarke 15 as a "pocket-sized parchment manuscript," which measures 102 x 88 mm. When extrapolating from his interpretation of the journeying metaphor found in the texts to the reality of a physical journey, he repeats and emphasizes that "the manuscript is pocket-sized: in other words, ideal to take with one when traveling."[10] The small page dimensions encourage one to imagine a 100 x 80 mm. pocket in a garment, suggesting the convenient portability of today's mobile phone or tablet. But, unlike such thin electronic devices, the 257 parchment leaves of this "small" manuscript create a considerable bulk and weight, so that the pocket in question would need not only to be considerably larger but quite sturdily reinforced as well. Although the binding in most surviving Greek manuscripts is not original, and the ornamented leather-stamped one of Clarke 15 is almost certainly somewhat later (figs. 1–2), it does in fact display one of the characteristic features of

---

10. Lauxtermann, "Perils," 202.

Figure 1.

Upper Board.
Oxford, Bodleian
Library, MS E. D.
Clarke 15.

(By permission of
the Bodleian Library,
Oxford University)

Figure 2.

Spine.
Oxford, Bodleian
Library, MS E. D.
Clarke 15.

(By permission of
the Bodleian Library,
Oxford University)

Barbara Crostini

Greek bindings, namely the raised headbands. These protruding leather flaps protecting the main sewing at either end of the spine, combined with its wooden boards, render this little codex highly unpocketable.

Rather than easily envisioning a medieval traveler slipping a volume into his or her pocket (notwithstanding the fact that medieval garments had no pockets![11]), the question of portability needs to be reformulated more broadly to ask just how manuscripts were carried about by travelers in the Middle Ages. As far as I know, this matter has not been investigated in detail for Greek manuscripts. In the West, the use of a special binding technique that transformed the leather covers into a book-bag, at once protecting the book and offering the carrier a means of tying this object to his/her belt or cart, is attested with examples extant from the thirteenth to the fifteenth centuries. Conservator Margit Smith has gathered all available evidence concerning the so-called girdle book.[12] Smith catalogued twenty-five extant exemplars in European and US collections. Although the number of surviving objects is small, additional testimony can be drawn from a wealth of art-historical depictions showing pilgrim travelers in action, or saints posing, with such girdle books. Since these books were undoubtedly made for travel, they should furnish some solid evidence as to size preference. However, the size of such objects reveals a surprising range, from very small

---

11. As was helpfully pointed out to me by an historian of medieval costume.

12. Margit J. Smith, *The Medieval Girdle Book* (Newcastle, DE, 2017). Dr. Smith talked about this research at the 38th Saint Louis Conference on Manuscript Studies (14–15 October 2011, Saint Louis University) and at the 15th Conference on the Care and Conservation of Manuscripts (2–4 April 2014, University of Copenhagen). Versions of these papers can be downloaded from the webpage: https://independent.academia.edu/MargitSmith. See also the article by J. A. Szirmai, "The Girdle Book of the Museum Meermanno-Westreenianum," *Quaerendo* 18 (1988): 17–34.

(63 x 47 mm.; Edinburgh, National Library of Scotland, Advocates MS 72.1.4) to rather large (738 x 217 mm.; Munich, Bayerische Staatsbibliothek, Cgm 8950). The latter volume contains a famous law collection and is presumably a traveling reference for judges whose job it was to go around the country administering the law. In fact, when considering florilegia manuscripts as handy travel reference for preachers, we are also dealing with large-sized volumes in need of special transport.

Two factors emerge when examining comparative evidence from Latin traveling codices in trying to establish criteria for identifying Greek manuscripts as traveling objects. The first is that size does not matter, strictly speaking, but rather it is the aptness of the structure of the volume (in particular, a special binding technique) that makes it fit for transport. The second point is that although sacred texts predominate in the contents of Latin girdle books, we may need to look at a wider range of *Gebrauchsliteratur* for signs indicative of the portability of a manuscript. One might object, however, that since the girdle binding technique is not attested in the East, and that, moreover, it is not found anywhere prior to the thirteenth century, size is still a good indication of portability. But other factors, too, should be considered before any small manuscript can be considered as primarily made for travel.

The level of production seems to be one of these additional factors that does not tally particularly well with a travel function hypothesis. As Lauxtermann notes, Clarke 15 is a deluxe codex. I was struck by this aspect in my inspection of the codex at the Bodleian Library. Although the parchment is not of absolutely top quality,[13] the use of gold

---

13. The parchment is of medium thickness, ivory-coloured, and skillfully prepared. The thickness of parchment could be interpreted either in support of or against a traveling hypothesis: thick parchment is resistant and can travel, but thin parchment diminishes bulk and weight.

to write page after page of epigrams in a large distinctive majuscule script known as *Auszeichnungsmajuskel*[14] (figs. 3–4) transmits a message of permanence and confident display, contrasting with the mood of agitation, displacement, and self-defense that Lauxtermann conjures out of his interpretation of the poems contained in the codex. According to Lauxtermann, "the manuscript [Mark the Monk] commissioned is emblematic of the dire straits he found himself in."[15] Even more dramatically, this volume was "a manuscript ... he took with him when he went on a journey from which he feared he would never return."[16] One may yet reflect whether, in practice, luxury and travel go well together, particularly when the traveler fears he may not return home. Paradigmatic qualities for a traveling manuscript could be its resistance, but also the plainness of its execution. As already precious objects in themselves, one could well imagine that the precarious conditions of travel would increase the chances of loss through damage, mishap, or theft.[17] The diminutive size and modest, pen-flourished decoration of London, British Library, Harley MS 5537 (s.xii, 117 x 90 mm.), for instance, would appear to be more appropriate qualities for a traveling book.[18]

On the other hand, the evidence points to the fact that precious execution goes in tandem with the choice of very small book format. Of the eighteen eleventh-century man-

---

14. Herbert Hunger, "Epigraphische Auszeichnungsmajuskel," *Jahrbuch der österreichischen Byzantinistik* 26 (1977): 193–210.

15. Lauxtermann, "Perils," 203.

16. Ibid., 202.

17. On book theft, for example, see Erik Kwakkel, "Chain, Chest, Curse: Combatting Book Theft in Medieval Times," Medievalbooks (blog) (10 July 2015), https://medievalbooks.nl/2015/07/10/chain-chest-curse-combating-book-theft-in-medieval-times/. Curses upon removers of books from monastic libraries were indeed common in Greek manuscripts.

18. See British Library, http://www.bl.uk/manuscripts/FullDisplay.aspx?ref=Harley_MS_5537.

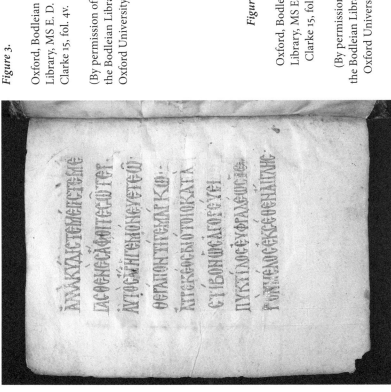

Figure 3.

Oxford, Bodleian Library, MS E. D. Clarke 15, fol. 4v.

(By permission of the Bodleian Library, Oxford University)

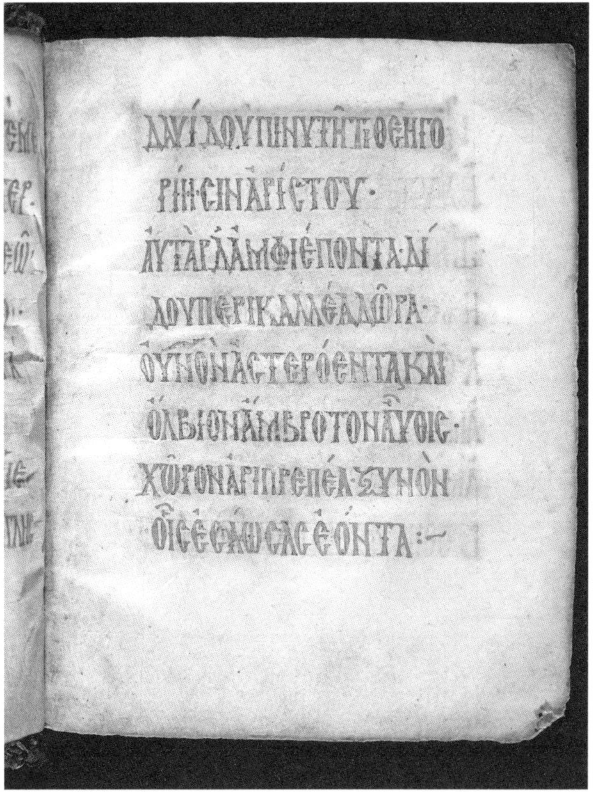

Figure 4.

Oxford, Bodleian Library, MS E. D. Clarke 15, fol. 5r.

(By permission of the Bodleian Library, Oxford University)

uscripts listed by Weyl Carr, comprising nine psalters and nine gospel books of small dimensions (under 120 mm. in height), twelve are noted as containing gold ink or ornament or both. Weyl Carr stresses the close link of the production of diminutive books—and more specifically of a cluster of psalters dated around the 1070s (thus including Clarke 15, which is more exactly dated by its Easter tables to 1077/78)—with imperial circles and patronage.[19] Despite the fact that the collaboration between scribes and painters of differing competence and talent produced objects of varying artistic quality,[20] Weyl Carr points to a close relation between Vatican City, Biblioteca Apostolica Vaticana, MS Vat. gr. 342, a psalter from 1087 measuring 180 x 130 mm., and the even smaller London, British Library, Add. MS 36928 from 1090, measuring 120 x 95 mm.[21] Their shared origin cannot be doubted when looking at the style and execution of the calendrical calculations and Easter tables: in both manuscripts, geometrical grids are drawn precisely by a double line in red ink, filled with gold and further ornamented by arabesque palmettes at the intersection of the pattern of circles.[22] The parallel is further confirmed by the iconographical scheme in the full-page miniature of David, set in an unusual, quadrilobe background.[23] While the Vatican psalter is undoubtedly connected with the capital, Constantinople, its close associate now at the British Library has been deemed to come from Palestine: it is thought to be a

19. Weyl Carr, "Diminutive Byzantine Manuscripts," 134.
20. Ibid., 131.
21. For Vat. gr. 342, see DigiVatLib, Biblioteca Apostolica Vaticana: https://digi.vatlib.it/view/MSS_Vat.lat.342; for Add. 36928, see British Library, http://www.bl.uk/manuscripts/FullDisplay.aspx?ref=Add_MS_36928.
22. Cf. esp. Vat. gr. 342, fols. 23r–23v; and Add. 36928, fols. 36v and 41v.
23. Vat. gr. 342, fol. 24v; Add. 36928, fol. 46v. Note that a quadrilobe frame is employed for the writing of Clarke 15, fol. 231v (fig. 5).

Figure 5.

Oxford, Bodleian Library, MS E. D. Clarke, fol. 231v.
(By permission of the Bodleian Library, Oxford University)

Barbara Crostini

provincial copy of an illustrious model.[24] Weyl Carr points out that it is not possible to reconstruct the precise dynamics of such exchanges. Thus, although she calls these two manuscripts "intimate relatives" of Clarke 15,[25] such close relationship need not determine identical provenance from the same scriptorium.

Clarke 15, however, is at one remove from the similarity between these two closer twins. Its Easter tables, though set in geometrical patterns of circles, are also enclosed in rectangular frames colored in red and blue and adorned with more usual Byzantine-style palmettes (figs. 6–7). It remains disputed whether the only extant figural full-page miniature in Clarke 15 is original to its creation or a later addition. Its poor state of conservation, with flaked, rubbed pigments and crude later restorations in thick red and black ink obscure the contents of the representation[26] and make the issue difficult to resolve. A greater homogeneity can be observed in the *mise-en-page*, especially that of Add. 36928, and specifically in the use of the margins for rubrics and titles, composed in metrical verses in the case of Clarke 15. Thus, despite some differences, and the continuing uncertainty as to their provenance, this group of eleventh-century Byzantine psalters of small proportions and high decorative ambition displays a coherence of form that points to a com-

---

24. Weyl Carr, "Diminutive Byzantine Manuscripts," 133 and n27. Anthony Cutler, "A Psalter from Mar Saba and the Evolution of the Byzantine David Cycle," *Journal of Jewish Art* 6 (1979): 39–63, argues for a Palestinian origin in terms of similarity with ancient monuments containing David cycles in that region. Also relevant is his pointing out (40 and nn14–16) that the computational wheels in this manuscript "derive from the *ordines intercalationis* of al-Bīrunī," who died in 1051. Thus, his text must have been received in an area not far from where he operated.

25. Weyl Carr, "Diminutive Byzantine Manuscripts," 133.

26. The seated scribe (fol. 10v) receiving a scroll from heaven, handed down by Christ, has been interpreted as an author portrait of David. Hutter, *Corpus*, 1:46–47, no. 32, and pls. 152–55, considers the image integral to the original production.

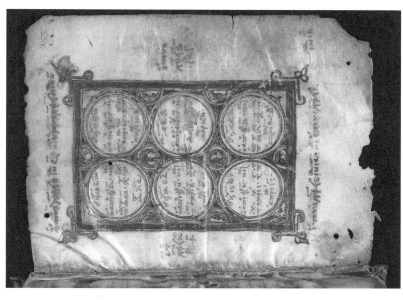

Figure 6.

Oxford, Bodleian Library, MS E. D. Clarke 15, fol. 254v.

(By permission of the Bodleian Library, Oxford University)

Figure 7.

Oxford, Bodleian Library, MS E. D. Clarke 15, fol. 255r.

(By permission of the Bodleian Library, Oxford University)

Barbara Crostini

monality of function, defined—also in view of their size—around the concept of private or personal devotion,[27] rather than in terms of traveling convenience.

The correlation between size and the production of psalters has been examined by John Lowden in comparing the size of illuminated psalters against the size of any type of pre-fifteenth-century manuscript from the library of the Vatopedi monastery on Mount Athos.[28] From his analysis, it appears that, while small formats are found across the board, psalters cluster markedly around the lower end of the spectrum, ranging from 100 to 200 mm. in height. Lowden concludes the results of this enquiry by stating that:

> ninety percent of these psalters are of modest to small, or very small, dimensions … The evidence is unambiguous: most psalters were small in comparison with the majority of Byzantine manuscripts … Indeed, before the mid-eleventh century, all surviving diminutive manuscripts are psalters.[29]

Lowden proceeds to reflect on the very question at the centre of this paper, namely "*why* most Byzantine psalters were deliberately made rather small."[30] He does not, however, conclude that small manuscripts were made for travel pur-

---

27. Weyl Carr, "Diminutive Byzantine Manuscripts," 133–34. See in general the contribution by Georgi Parpulov, "Psalters and Personal Piety in Byzantium," in *The Old Testament in Byzantium*, ed. Paul Magdalino and Robert Nelson (Washington, DC, 2010), 77–106. Parpulov underlines the textual distinctiveness of psalter paratexts as marking special commissions according to the sponsor/owner's tastes. Miniatures added for meditative purposes are another sign of function. Large, rather than small, size probably marks institutional ownership, although this is hardly attested by ownership marks (see esp. 82–83).
28. John Lowden, "Observations on Illustrated Byzantine Psalters," *Art Bulletin* 70 (1988): 242–60 at 245–48 and fig. 3.
29. Ibid., 245, 247.
30. Ibid., 247.

Perils of Travel

poses, but rather contemplates the value of portability more broadly in the context of daily local movement. While travelers such as high-ranking ecclesiastics or bishops on missions are possible bearers (although, as Lowden observes, "they should have known the Psalter by heart" and therefore did not need it written down at all), they might equally have been people, perhaps women,

> who had no intention of traveling long distances, but who merely wanted to carry the psalter about with them, perhaps from room to room, or from house to church.[31]

This emphasis on local movement would have been equally apt within the space of the monastic enclosure that, despite its limitations, was nevertheless not without complexity in its dynamics as a purpose-designated environment.[32]

The shape of the psalter book was partly established by tradition, determining an average size in the lower ranges of book format, while, according to Lowden, the few oversized volumes were due to extraordinary levels of patronage, as in the case of the imperially sponsored Psalter of Basil II (Venice, Biblioteca Nazionale Marciana, MS gr. 17).[33] The ordinariness of small sizes from 150 to 200 mm.

---

31. Ibid.

32. The complexity is such that current attempts at envisaging monastic space as a network of mobility have adopted a topological model for analysis. See Ekaterini Mitsiou, "The Defensive Character of Monastic Space: A Topological Analysis" (paper presented at the conference, *From the Human Body to the Universe: Spatialities of Byzantine Culture*, Uppsala University, 18–21 May 2017). Mitsiou's work is part of the project on "Mobility, Microstructures and Personal Agency in Byzantium," directed by Claudia Rapp (https://rapp.univie.ac.at/fileadmin/user_upload/p_rapp/Events_2018/Flyer__Wittgenstein_-_29.6.2018.pdf).

33. Lowden, "Observations," 246. Other large volumes included catena commentaries, such as Vienna, Österreichische Nationalbibliothek, MS

Barbara Crostini

in height does not diminish the exceptional nature of very small manuscripts between 90 and 120 mm. in height. Using the measurements recorded by Georgi Parpulov in his study of psalter manuscripts,[34] I have extracted a list of eleventh- and twelfth-century manuscripts of "ordinary" small size yielding a total of 239 items, of which only twenty-one manuscripts are of exceptionally small format, while the bulk of the codices groups, as expected, in the middle range.[35]

---

theol. gr. 8; or Vatican City, Biblioteca Apostolica Vaticana, MS Vat. gr. 752.

34. Georgi R. Parpulov, *Toward a History of Byzantine Psalters, ca. 850–1350 AD* (Plovdiv, 2014), https://archive.org/details/ByzPsalters.

35. Very small manuscripts not listed in Weyl Carr, "Diminutive Byzantine Manuscripts," include: Athens, National Bank of Greece Cultural Foundation, MS Pezarou 50 (110 x 90 mm., s.xi[ex]); Mt. Athos, Dionysiou Monastery, MS 585 (130 x 90 mm., s.xi), perhaps the same as Mt. Athos, Dionysiou Monastery, MS 565 (s.xii) in Weyl Carr, "Diminutive Byzantine Manuscripts," 153; Mt Athos, Kausokalybion Monastery, MS 87 (100 x 70 mm., s.xi, now lost); Mt. Athos, Great Lavra Monastery, MS B 12 (110 x 100 mm., s.xi); Mt. Athos, Vatopedi Monastery MS 1231 (110 x 80 mm., s.xi[ex]); Besançon, Bibliothèque municipale, MS 33 (130 x 90 mm., 1056); Florence, Biblioteca Medicea Laurenziana, MS Conv. soppr. 36 (120 x 100 mm., s.xi); London, British Library, Add. MS 40731 (110 x 90 mm., s.xi, "Bristol Psalter"); London, British Library, Royal MS 2.A.vi (110 x 80 mm., s.xii[in], parchment mounted on paper, with very large script); Milan, Biblioteca Ambrosiana, MS B 1 sup. (120 x 90 mm., s.xii); Oxford, Bodleian Library, MS Canon. gr. 114 (110 x 80 mm., s.xii); Oxford, Bodleian Library, MS Wake 44 (70 x 60 mm., s.xi); Mt. Sinai, Monastery of Saint Catherine, MS gr. 2054 (100 x 80 mm., s.xii); and St. Petersburg, Russian National Library, MS gr. 348 (100 x 80 mm, s.xii). Differences in dating include: Florence, Biblioteca Medicea Laurenziana, MS Conv. soppr. 35 is dated s.xi by Weyl Carr, "Diminutive Byzantine Manuscripts," 154, but s.xii by Parpulov, *Toward a History of Byzantine Psalters*, Appendix; Milan, Biblioteca Trivulziana, MS 340 is dated s.xiii by Parpulov, *Toward a History of Byzantine Psalters*, Appendix, but s.xii by Weyl Carr, "Diminutive Byzantine Manuscripts," 154; Paris, Bibliothèque nationale de France, MS Par. gr. 41 is dated s.xii by Weyl Carr, "Diminutive Byzantine Manuscripts," 153, but s.xi by Parpulov, *Toward a History of Byzantine Psalters*,

Perils of Travel

If the whole range of measurements between 100 and 200 mm. in height could be equally portable in regard to the qualification as a travel manuscript, another observation by Lowden seems to me to be more pertinent for these extremely small formats, namely that "there was probably also an element of curiosity value in a book only some 10 cm tall."[36] This statement I interpret to mean not that these diminutive books were without function, but that their *raison d'être* consisted in their being the very opposite of practical; rather, it was their qualities as exotic, curious, small, and precious objects that contributed to their symbolic value. Reduction in size does not correspond simply to the production of smaller and, therefore, less expensive copies of the same book.[37] Instead, such volumes lent themselves to being given as gifts on special occasions, which explains why they contain both standard elements, such as the repertoire of verses, and singular aspects arising from the specificity of their commission. As I shall argue in the remaining

---

Appendix; and Mt. Sinai, Monastery of Saint Catherine, MSS gr. 64 and 65 are dated s.xii by Weyl Carr, "Diminutive Byzantine Manuscripts," 153, but postdated by Parpulov, *Toward a History of Byzantine Psalters*, Appendix. Summary of measurements in height: 30 codices above 300 mm., 35 codices below 300 mm., 59 codices below 250 mm., 62 codices below 200 mm., and 52 codices below 150 mm. Summary of measurements in width: 46 codices above 200 mm., 76 codices below 200 mm., 95 codices below 150 mm., and 21 codices between 80 and 90 mm. Parpulov, of course, had more detailed catalogues available and greater access to Mt. Athos than Weyl Carr, but the comparison between these lists also shows a discrepancy in dating I am unable to assess here.

36. Lowden, "Observations," 247.

37. See Robert S. Nelson and Jerry L. Bona, "Relative Size and Comparative Value in Byzantine Illuminated Manuscripts: Some Quantitative Perspectives," in *Paleografia e codicologia greca: Atti del II Colloquio internazionale (Berlino-Wolfenbüttel, 17–21 ottobre 1983)*, ed. Dieter Harlfinger and Giancarlo Prato (Alessandria, 1991), 339–53 at 351. No truly diminutive format is included in Nelson and Bona's discussion, with the exception of London, British Library, Add. MS 40753, a twelfth-century psalter, whose relationship to the group presented is not sufficiently drawn out.

part of this paper, diminutive psalters were a particularly suitable gift for entry into monastic life, and this journey from the world to a retreated existence within a community was appropriately marked and mirrored in the contents of such psalters. It is this metaphorical journey attendant to the change of status that the poems in Clarke 15 eloquently celebrate.

LAUXTERMANN'S TRAVELING HYPOTHESIS: A QUESTION OF SALVATION

Lauxtermann's argument in favour of an actual physical journey is based not only on the size of the codex—though this factor is taken as decisive—but also on the analysis of three specific passages in the verses contained in the manuscript and attributed to the same Mark the Monk to whom the codex is dedicated.[38] The obscurity of this otherwise unknown author[39] contrasts with the evaluation of his verses as sophisticated in terms of language and style. As Lauxtermann declares:

> it is doubtless the work of a highbrow author and it must have cost him many years of thorough linguistic training to attain the stylistic level of pseudo-Homeric and pseudo-Attic Greek he displays in his poems, and seemingly without any effort.[40]

---

38. For a complete list of the poems contained in Clarke 15 and the transcription of their texts, see the Database of Byzantine Book Epigrams, http://www.dbbe.ugent.be/manuscript/view/id/20.

39. His attestation in the eleventh-century Clarke 15 anticipates by two centuries the attempts to identify this Mark the Monk with some thirteenth-century homonymous poets: see F. Ciccolella, "Carmi anacreontici bizantini," *Bollettino dei classici*, 3rd ser., 12 (1991): 49–68 at 55 and nn5–6.

40. Lauxtermann, "Perils," 200.

Perils of Travel

The copious notes on classical literary echoes with which Stefec supplies his edition of Mark's main poems go some way towards demonstrating the complexity of these verses.[41] However, the intricate web of intertextual references that lies beneath the surface of these apparently simple poems has yet to be fully explored. Without aspiring to a full analysis here, a reconsideration of the passages discussed in Lauxtermann's article should at least open up some avenues for future research.

Lauxtermann does not deny that where the motif of the journey is mentioned in the verses this may well be a spiritual, rather than a physical, reference. Nevertheless, he cannot abandon his main thesis regarding this purpose-made manuscript and presents Mark ready to march out of the monastic walls clutching his precious psalter. Lauxtermann goes as far as to speculate on the aim of this journey, perhaps some specific mission, and graphically expounds on the real dangers of the highways in Mark's own times.[42] This enjoyable fiction is based on his identifying one portion of Mark's poem as falling "in the category of ἐνόδια, prayers said when one goes on a journey."[43] In two further verses, "[a]lthough Mark the Monk obviously refers … to a spiritual journey, his choice of vocabulary seems to suggest that the prospect of an actual journey is also on his mind."[44]

Finally, the parable of the lost sheep (Luke 15:1–7) with which Mark identifies his predicament in his personal prayer to Sabas, perhaps his spiritual father, is decoded by Lauxtermann as a metaphor indicating real travel because of the convenient pocket-sized format of this manuscript,

---

41. Rudolf Stefec, "Anmerkungen zu weiteren Epigrammen in epigraphischer Auszeichnungsmajuskel," *Byzantion* 81 (2011): 326–61, esp. 343–48. Stefec's edition appeared at precisely the same time as Lauxtermann's article, without either being aware.
42. Lauxtermann, "Perils," 202–3.
43. Ibid., 201.
44. Ibid., 202.

as discussed above. Mark may be going on a journey, perhaps being sent on a specific mission by his abbot, but—Lauxtermann ponders—"he is lost. He has wandered off ... But where has he gone?"[45] Let us pick up these three traveling threads one by one.

The first clue to the traveling nature of Clarke 15 is signaled by Lauxtermann in the final lines of the first introductory poem written on fols. 3r–5v, verses 12–19. According to Lauxtermann, the verb ἡγεμόνευε designates Mark's prayer here as belonging to the genre of hexametric *enodia*, "prayers said when one goes on a journey." The verses in question read:

> ἀλλὰ κύδιστε μέγιστε μεγασθενὲς ἄφθιτε σῶτερ
> αὐτὸς ἄρ᾽ ἡγεμόνευε τεῷ θεράποντί γε Μάρκῳ
> ἀτρεκέος βιότοιο κατὰ στίβον ὡς ἀγορεύῃ
> πυκτίδος εὐφραδέως ἱερὸν μέλος ἐκ σέθεν αἴγλης
> Δαυίδου πινυτῆτι θεηγορίῃσιν ἀρίστου·
> αὐτὰρ δ᾽ ἀμφιέποντα· δίδου περικαλλέα δῶρα·
> οὐρανὸν ἀστερόεντα καὶ ὄλβιον ἄμβροτον αὖθις·
> χῶρον ἀριπρεπέα· ξυνὸν οἷς ἐσάωσας ἐόντα.[46]

> But o most noble and great, o mighty imperishable Saviour
> You yourself lead your servant Mark
> along the path of a strict lifestyle so that he may proclaim
> from this sacred book the holy song of David who is the best in wise talk about the divine from the radiance (that comes) from you.

---

45. Ibid., 202.

46. Stefec, "Anmerkungen," 340. Stefec reads ἐν σέθεν αἴγλης at ln. 15 and has a full stop at ln. 16 (ἀρίστου). I have added the upper points where Clarke 15 displays such punctuation marks. See Database of Byzantine Book Epigrams, http://www.dbbe.ugent.be/occurrence/view/id/36/.

And grant as most beautiful gifts round about:
a starry sky and god-like happiness back
to the high place, in common with those whom you have saved.[47]

In this prayer, the Saviour (i.e., Christ, not God) is invoked to guide his servant Mark along the path of true life. I can see nothing unusual in such a prayer as marking Mark's submission to a guide in his journey to salvation. In fact, the abbot or *hegoumenos* is probably the figure who takes on the role of Christ in Mark's human experience at this point, since it is Mark's joining of a monastic community that is clearly at stake here. In his analysis, Lauxtermann incidentally discusses the possible reasons for making a monastic profession and incisively puts forward the hypothesis "that political turmoil of some kind certainly contributed to Mark's decision to don the habit."[48]

However, in pursuing his traveling hypothesis, Lauxtermann needs to posit that Mark has taken leave of (rather than joined) his community and is expressing through this prayer his desire to return. As Lauxtermann states:

Mark prays to God "to guide him along the path of true life" … and to "grant him the splendid gifts that will accompany him, namely the starry heavens and, on his return (αὖθις), the bright place shared with others, prosperous and immortal, wherewith Thou savest mortal beings." The bright place shared with others, of course, is Mark's monastery. But what about the starry heavens? And why should God "guide (Mark)"?[49]

---

47. My translation. With thanks to Professor Anastasia Maravela for valuable suggestions in this and the following passages.
48. Lauxtermann, "Perils," 201.
49. Ibid.

Barbara Crostini

Lauxtermann's overly literal reading of an established poetic topos associated with travel leads him to jump quickly to conclusions: he thinks of Mark out in the open (under starry heavens) and of a journey in which splendid gifts "accompany him" (ἀμφιέποντα) back (αὖθις) to the community (χῶρον … ξυνὸν). But is this the correct interpretation of these final lines? Or is Lauxtermann bending the meaning of these verses to fit his hypothesis of Clarke 15 as a book intended for travel?

Although the meaning of the adjective ἀμφιέποντα, with its likely adverbial force, is unclear (perhaps "enveloping" as a garment?), what is beyond doubt is the evocation here of a paradisiacal landscape as a place of happiness, with a starry vault, where those who have been saved abide. Besides its Homeric origin, this evocation of the οὐρανὸν ἀστερόεντα calls to mind the sky represented on the verso of the tenth-century Harbaville Triptych now in the Louvre as typical of the Paradisiacal Garden that grows below it.[50] In the hymns of Romanos Melodos, the absence of luminaries signifies Hell, where stars fall like leaves, one by one.[51] The company that this traveler wants to join is that of the community of saints for whom Heaven is assured.

This primary meaning does not, of course, entirely obviate the possibility that an earthly, concrete community could also be in the mind of the spiritual traveler when using the established and quite common metaphor of the monastery as Paradise,[52] but the reference passes through

---

50. Musée du Louvre, https://www.louvre.fr/en/oeuvre-notices/harbaville-triptych (with thanks to Basema Hamarneh for bringing this object to my attention).

51. Romanos le Mélode, "Hymn des dix vierges," strophe 5, in Romanos le Mélode, *Hymnes*, ed. José Grosdidier de Matons, 5 vols., Sources chrétiennes 99, 110, 114, 128, 283 (Paris, 1964–81), 5:271–327 at 303–5. Thanks to Thomas Arentzen for providing this reference.

52. On this theme, see Giles Constable, "Renewal and Reform in Religious Life: Concepts and Realities," in *Renaissance and Renewal in the*

the metaphor rather than the other way round. If Mark is not to be envisioned wandering about the countryside on his departure, only longing to return safely to the monastery later on, another interpretation needs to be given to the adverb, αὖθις, which on its own also bears much responsibility for this traveling vignette. I suggest that it should be read as marking a temporal, rather than a spatial, transition: the emphasis is on "again, anew" rather than on "back, back again." Since the occasion hypothesized is that of Mark's joining a community, the adverb signals, in effect, that this is "Mark's" second entry into monastic life. This circumstance is what makes the occasion celebrated by these verses more turbulent than most. And it may well be, as Lauxtermann suggests, that the contingent causes for this return were not entirely out of free will or independent of changing political circumstances.

A look at the intertextual echoes of these sophisticated verses creates a tantalizing background to this story of a second conversion. As Stefec notes, these lines are full of common Homeric phrases such as περικαλλέα δῶρα and οὐρανὸν ἀστερόεντα. The verb form ἐσάωσας also belongs to the type of Homeric archaism privileged by these compositions: there are only six occurrences of this lexical form in the *Thesaurus linguae Graecae*. But rather than a primary reference to Homer, I suggest that another significant Christian text is being consciously alluded to here. For all these lexemes frequently occur in the fourth-century poet Eudocia Augusta, as exemplified in this prayer from her liturgical composition, *De sancto Cypriano*:

πάντων δεσπόζων, θεὲ κύδιμε, παιδὸς ἀχράντου
Ἰησοῦ Χριστοῦ γενέτα, ὃς ταρταρόεντα
αἰνοπέλωρον ὄφιν ζοφεραῖς ἐπέδησας ἐν αὐλαῖς,

Twelfth Century, ed. Robert L. Benson and Giles Constable (Cambridge, MA, 1982), 37–67 at 48–49.

Barbara Crostini

οὓς δὲ πέδαις ζώγρησεν, ὅλους, κύδιστ', ἐσάωσας·
ὃς πόλον ἀστερόεντα τανυσσάμενος σέο χειρί,
γῆν δὲ μέσον χάεος νοτίοις νώτοισιν ἐρείσας.[53]

In this prayer, Cyprian's female victim, Justina, appeals for God's help in rejecting yet another lustful attack by the devil. In order not to succumb, she proclaims her love for Christ, makes the sign of the cross, and invokes God's help through these lines that recognize God's power over all Creation. The Christianization of the Homeric motifs in the eleventh-century verses of Clarke 15 has been processed through fourth-century authors such as Eudocia, who are this poet's true models. The currency of Eudocia's work as an intellectual reference point and a source for contemporary Byzantine poetry is neatly witnessed by an eleventh-century copy of her poem. In Florence, Biblioteca Medicea Laurenziana, MS Plut. 7.10, her work has been copied together with the other great poet, Gregory Nazianzen, and with Nonnus of Panopolis.[54] In this working copy, some of the verses have been intensely annotated in the margins by a contemporary scholarly hand.[55]

---

53. Arthur Ludwich, *Eudociae Augustae, Procli Lycii, Claudiani carminum Graecorum reliquiae* (Leipzig, 1897), 29–30, ll. 64–69; an Italian translation is provided by Claudio Bevegni, *Eudocia Augusta: Storia di San Cipriano* (Milan, 2006), 89. My thanks to the Patristic Seminar, Newman Institute, Uppsala, and in particular to Marianne Wifstrand Schiebe for discussion of this passage.

54. This copy is one of the most ancient, complete, and authoritative for these authors: see Jean Irigoin, *Tradition et critique des textes grecs* (Paris, 1997), 97. The manuscript is fully digitized at Teca Digitale Laurenziana, http://opac.bmlonline.it/Record.htm?record=736012455429.

55. See, for example, Plut. 7.10, fol. 8r. Although a comparison has been suggested with Florence, Biblioteca Medicea Laurenziana, MS Plut. 32.9 (Sophocles), the angularity of the script in this case is not a sign of an earlier date (s.x) but rather appears to denote the scribe's freedom with respect to parameters of calligraphic *Perlschrift*: see Myriam Hec-

Perils of Travel

If the use of Eudocia as a source is fitting for the intellectual circles of eleventh-century Constantinople, which considered her work both an inspiration for the contents and a lexical reservoir for their literary aims, allusion to the Life of Cyprian of Antioch in the Clarke poem may take on further significance in view of the context of conversion just sketched out. Cyprian's conversion from the magical arts to Christianity via the renunciation of the erotic powers of seduction[56] might have been considered especially appropriate as a paradigm for conversion for Mark the Monk also. Intertextual allusions to this text work as a coded metaphor for the situation of the author and composer of the Clarke poem. In the context of a second profession, therefore, it is likely that the name "Mark" should also function as a pseudonym, as a (or another) monastic name for the real name of the author. This change would go some way towards explaining why we have no record of the high-level poet Mark in eleventh-century Byzantium, a fact that Lauxtermann himself considered puzzling. Thus, a web of literary references in the poems could be seen as a coded message alluding to the veiled authorship.

Lauxtermann's first piece of textual evidence in support of his view of Clarke 15 as a manuscript made for travel, contextualizing it within the genre of *enodia*, is not supported by the interpretation here discussed. The travel alluded to is primarily a journey of salvation, and the metaphor works well only in the context of "Mark's" actually

---

quert-Devienne, "Lecture nouvelle d'Oedipus roi de Sophocle dans les mss L et A," *Revue d'histoire des textes* 24 (1994): 1–60.

56. For a good introduction to this legend and its transmission, see Ryan Bailey, "The *Confession* of Cyprian of Antioch: Introduction, Text and Translation" (PhD diss., MacGill University, Montreal, 2009), 21–23, for Eudocia's version (see http://digitool.library.mcgill.ca/webclient/StreamGate?folder_id=0&dvs=1555096972498~443). The other allusion to this text is in Gregory Nazianzen's *Oration* 24 (see Bailey, "*Confession* of Cyprian*,*" 18–19).

once again joining a community, as marked by these verses. However, the troubles perceived by Lauxtermann may well have been actual, and could appropriately refer to a journey of conversion experienced by this individual whose highly sophisticated poetic skills were applied to create significant resonances between his literary verses and his actual predicament.

The second passage in which Lauxtermann detects evidence of traveling activity, and specifically "the motive for the journey," is found in verses 25–30 of the third introductory poem to the manuscript.[57] As Lauxtermann states:

> Here we read that the true believer, when he reads and sings the Psalter, will reap spiritual salvation and, I quote, "will most definitely walk the path that leads to heaven, without erring and with determined pace." Although Mark the Monk obviously refers here to a spiritual journey, his choice of vocabulary seems to suggest that the prospect of an actual journey is also on his mind.[58]

While the spiritual aspiration in question can hardly be doubted here, since ψυχικὴν σωτηρίαν is mentioned at v. 28, the renewed claim concerning a corresponding physical journey is not accompanied by any detailed analysis of the "choice of vocabulary" used.

Let us therefore inspect the last two verses for such practical language:

τρυγῶν ἀληθῶς ψυχικὴν σ(ωτη)ρίαν
καὶ τὴν ἄνω φέρουσαν ἀπλανῆ τρίβον
εὐθυβόλῳ μάλιστα βαδίζων τάχει.

---

57. Stefec, "Anmerkungen," 345–46; see Plut. 7.10, fol. 9r.
58. Lauxtermann, "Perils," 201–2.

Perils of Travel

And he will truly reap the salvation of the soul and
he will most definitely walk with steady speed the
straight path leading upwards.[59]

The "path without strayings" indirectly suggests the opposite context (i.e., one where diversions have indeed happened). But does the noun τρίβον, with or without its qualifier ἀπλανῆ, call for a practical rather than a metaphorical journeying? The most obvious reference is to Isaiah 3:12:

λαός μου, οἱ πράκτορες ὑμῶν καλαμῶνται ὑμᾶς,
καὶ οἱ ἀπαιτοῦντες κυριεύουσιν ὑμῶν· λαός μου, οἱ
μακαρίζοντες ὑμᾶς <u>πλανῶσιν</u> ὑμᾶς καὶ τὸν <u>τρίβον</u>
τῶν ποδῶν ὑμῶν ταράσσουσιν.

O my people, your exactors strip you, and extortioners rule over you: O my people, they that pronounce you blessed lead you astray, and pervert the path of your feet.[60]

This verse not only refers to a non-literal context for the act of walking as a metaphor for righteousness, but also sets the scene within a specific type of self-delusion caused by flattery. While the blessedness of fame is deceitful, the humility of monastic choice (for example) guarantees a more truthful and worthwhile (self-)esteem.

Another example is Psalm 77:50 (LXX)

---

59. Translation by Klaas Bentein and Kristoffel Demoen, "The Reader in Eleventh-Century Book Epigrams," in *Poetry and its Contexts*, 69–88 at 84–85; also at http://www.dbbe.ugent.be/type/view/id/2128/.
60. *The Septuagint Version of the Old Testament, with an English Translation and with Various Readings and Critical Notes*, ed. Lancelot Brenton (London, 1879), 838.

Barbara Crostini

ὡδοποίησε <u>τρίβον</u> τῇ ὀργῇ αὐτοῦ καὶ οὐκ ἐφείσατο
ἀπὸ θανάτου τῶν ψυχῶν αὐτῶν καὶ τὰ κτήνη αὐτῶν
εἰς θάνατον συνέκλεισε.

He made a way for his wrath; he spared not their
souls from death, but consigned their cattle to
death.[61]

It cannot be the question of a real, concrete road used to
convey God's anger, but one where the images of destruction and salvation meet in metaphor. It is worth remembering one of the following verses in this psalm (vv. 52–53):

καὶ ἀπῆρεν ὡς πρόβατα τὸν λαὸν αὐτοῦ καὶ
ἀνήγαγεν αὐτοὺς ὡσεὶ ποίμνιον ἐν ἐρήμῳ / καὶ
ὡδήγησεν αὐτοὺς ἐπ' ἐλπίδι.

And he removed his people like sheep; he led them as
a flock in the wilderness. / And he guided them with
hope.[62]

This passage serves to continue the image to its conclusion and to point forward to the next inscription in the manuscript, which refers precisely to lost sheep.

A polysemic use of τρίβον ἀσφαλῆ occurs at Wisdom 14:3 in a highly charged metaphorical construction, where shipwreck and last-chance salvation are dramatically intertwined with questions of correct belief, worship, and moral conduct.[63] Next to such specific biblical occurrences of this lemma, it is important to underline more generally the currency of "the idea of sin as a deviation from a path or

---

61. Ibid., 745.
62. Ibid.
63. The whole passage is Wisdom 14:1–7. Further work is necessary to establish its currency and use in Byzantium.

direction" that was embedded in the Old Testament understanding of moral failure as "failure to reach a goal." As Joseph Lam well recapitulates:

> Whether it is because of the implicitly goal-directed character of the moral life as commonly conceived, or because of the coherence between the properties of spatial movement and typical conceptions of life progress, metaphors of path lend themselves well to the language of morality of which sin is a part.[64]

Thus, a priori in the biblical context and even more in that of a psalter manuscript, travel is not only obviously metaphorical, but also appropriately chosen as the standard frame of reference for spiritual progress or failure.

If we turn to the Church Fathers, we find that both Theodoret and Cyril (the latter twice[65]) adopt this combination of adjective and noun to refer to clearly spiritual journeys. In Theodoret, the "road" is one of enlightenment, whereas in Cyril the road is that "of the saints" and it is a road "of faith."[66] Finally, in the liturgical context of the canons celebrating the forty-two martyrs of Amorion for 6 March, the

---

64. Joseph Lam, *Patterns of Sin in the Hebrew Bible: Metaphor, Culture, and the Making of a Religious Concept* (Oxford, 2016), 156, and see generally chp. 4 "Sin as Path or Direction."

65. See also references in Stefec, "Anmerkungen," 347, for Cyril of Alexandria, *Commentarius in Isaiam*: Maurice Geerard, ed., *Clavis partum graecorum*, 7 vols. (Turnhout, 1974–2018), 3:3, no. 5203; Jacques-Paul Migne, *Patrologiae cursus completus ... series graeca*, 161 vols. (Paris, 1857–66), 70:636, ln. 17.

66. References from Thesaurus linguae Graecae: Theodoret, *De providentia orationes decem* [4089.032], vol. 83, p. 716, ln. 12: φωταγωγούμενοι καὶ ποδηγούμενοι τῷ τούτων βίῳ / καὶ λόγῳ, τὴν ἀπλανῆ τρίβον οὕτω πως ὁδεύωσιν; Cyril Alex., *De incarnatione unigeniti* [4090.026], ed. Autbert p. 681, ln. 2: τὴν δὲ ἀπλανῆ τῶν ἁγίων διάττοντας τρίβον ἐπ' αὐτὴν ἰέναι τὴν ἀλήθειαν; Cyril Alex., *Quod unus sit Christus* [4090.027], ed. Autbert p. 740, ln. 26: τὴν ἀπλανῆ τῆς πίστεως βαδιούμεθα τρίβον.

ἀπλανῆ τρίβον is that of their martyrdom.[67] Thus, neither the noun nor its epithet stand in support of the concrete interpretation suggested by Lauxtermann.

Lastly, the adjective εὐθυβόλῳ, meaning "to throw in a straight line," does not appear bound by a physical meaning either, since it is mostly used (at least in the dative) by Philo in a metaphorical way, about casting or projecting one's voice; in John Chrysostom, it is also used of sailing in a straight line, a specific activity that gets picked up in dictionary definitions.[68] In fact, water imagery in these verses could perhaps cumulatively be taken as furnishing some indication of the location of Mark's monastery, if it were not itself a very common vehicle for metaphorical meaning.

As for the verb βαδίζων, it is very commonly used, and normally with the adverbs ταχέως/ταχὺ. I doubt one can hang much on this choice, except that one usage by Psellos in a little poem contemporary to that in our manuscript uses such combination if not properly as a metaphor, at least with a good deal of extended meaning: Peter moves quickly to spread the Gospel of Jesus, as if with wings.[69]

In conclusion, the "vocabulary" chosen in these verses fits well with the tenor of biblical language and patristic in-

---

67. Canon for the 42 Martyrs of Amorion (6 March), in *Analecta hymnica graeca e codicibus eruta Italiae inferioris*, ed. G. Schirò and E. Tomadakis (Rome, 1971), 89, ll. 76–85: Ἐν φυλακῇ / πεπεδημένος τοὺς πόδας σου τῷ σιδήρῳ, / Κάλλιστε ἀήττητε,/ τοῦ μαρτυρίου τὴν ἀπλανῆ/ τρίβον διοδεῦσαι/ ἀνεμποδίστως ἱκέτευες·/ λυθεὶς δὲ διὰ ξίφους / ἐκ τοῦ σώματος αὖθις/ τῇ στοργῇ συνεδέθης τοῦ κτίσαντος. The expression recurs in other liturgical refrains also.

68. E.g., Hesychius of Alexandria, *Hesychii Alexandrini lexicon*, ed. Kurt Latte, alt. ed. by Ian Cunningham (Berlin, 2018), s.v.: ἐπ' εὐθείας βάλλοντι ἢ πλέοντι. ἢ εὐθυβόλῳ, ἀντὶ τοῦ συνετῷ.

69. Michael Psellos, *Michaelis Pselli poemata*, ed. Leendert Gerrit Westerink (Stuttgart, 1992), 458, poem 82: Ὁ Χριστὸς πρὸς τὸν Πέτρον / Εἰ συμμεριστής, εἰ μαθητής μου θέλεις, / Πέτρε, καλεῖσθαι καὶ †μαθητὴς† καὶ φίλος / πάντως σε νίψω· καὶ πτερωθεὶς ἐν τάχει / βάδιζε καὶ κήρυττε κόσμῳ παντί με.

terpretation that systematically employs traveling metaphors to refer to spiritual journeying. To insinuate another level of significance would require at the minimum a more extensive linguistic argumentation than that provided in Lauxtermann's article.

The third piece of evidence used by Lauxtermann is a particular poem, a prayer inserted in the manuscript after Psalm 76 (fol. 130r), whose metaphorical language is taken to provide the conclusive evidence for "real journeying." Lauxtermann states that:

> this time [Mark] is praying to his spiritual father Sabbas, probably the abbot of the monastery he is living in. He asks him to take care of him, just as the good shepherd did, when he looked for the sheep that had gone astray … This prayer is without parallel in Byzantine poetry and bears witness, to say the least, to a rather agitated state of mind. The important thing to note is that Mark the Monk once again makes use of metaphors and similes that seem to indicate that he is on his way to somewhere. He is lost. He has wandered off just as the lamb inadvertently wandered off from its herd and had to be rescued by the good shepherd. It is clear that Mark the Monk wants to return to the flock. But where has he gone? Where is this lamb of God? At this point we should remember the size of the manuscript. As stated above, the manuscript is pocket-sized: in other words, ideal to take with one when traveling.[70]

---

70. Lauxtermann, "Perils," 202. Lauxtermann (205n33) confesses that he does not "fully understand line 3 of the second poem." I do understand what it is that Lauxtermann does not understand. Why does he introduce the name "Sabaites" in a context where the poem names only a single Sabas and his homonym (St. Sabas)? And what has a reference to Psellos's enemies to do with this?

Barbara Crostini

The placement of the poem should alert us to the tailored nature of its contents. Psalm 76 (77):20 ends with the words, ὡδήγησας ὡς πρόβατα τὸν λαόν σου ἐν χειρὶ Μωϋσῆ καὶ Ἀαρών (Thou didst guide thy people as sheep by the hand of Moses and Aaron), which is not only the immediate prompt for the metaphor used, but also provides additional information about the context of strife in which this heartfelt prayer was set. Sirarpie Der Nersessian has pointed out in the case of the Theodore Psalter, which visualizes this psalm verse in an elaborate sheep-full full-page illumination (fol. 99v), that the symbolic import of Moses and Aaron is that of the struggle between spiritual and temporal powers.[71] Here, the authority of the abbot over his lost sheep is re-asserted over and above some other authority that has taken hold of it/him in a worldly situation. Again this trouble fits in well with the context of a second profession. One might also reflect on the line θηρσὶν φονῶσιν εἰς βορὰν εἰλημμένον· (the fate of being devoured by bloodthirsty beasts) to look for the type of threat that might have actively menaced the monk before he found (renewed) refuge in this coenobium. Psellos's mysterious and surely highly allusive leopard springs to mind.[72]

Prosopographical knowledge about people named Sabas has advanced since Lauxtermann checked,[73] and now at least

---

71. Sirarpie Der Nersessian, *L'illustration des psautiers grecs du Moyen Âge*, vol. 2, *Londres, Add. 19.352* (Paris, 1970), 86; see also Barbara Crostini, "Navigando per il Salterio: riflessioni intorno all'edizione elettronica del manoscritto Londra, British Library, Addit. 19.352, Seconda parte: Il significato storico del Salterio di Teodoro," *Bollettino della Badia greca di Grottaferrata* 56–57 (2002–3), 133–209 at 145–46.

72. See Michael Jeffreys and Marc D. Lauxtermann, eds., *The Letters of Psellos: Cultural Networks and Historical Realities* (Oxford, 2017), 5 and 260–61.

73. Lauxtermann, "Perils," 199–200 and 200n23 declares not to have found any records.

Perils of Travel

three records can be found online.[74] All three are attested in the second half of the eleventh century and are associated to monasteries. Sabas, *hegoumenos* of the Vatopedi Monastery on Mt. Athos, is mentioned in a decree from Xenophontos Monastery when Alexios I ordered that the latter monastery be returned to its exiled hegoumenos Symeon in 1089. Sabas, *grammatikos* and monk at the Iviron Monastery, is recorded in connection with disputed monastic properties on the border with Macedonia and interacted with Patriarch John Xiphilinos on such matters in 1071. And Sabas, monk and *protosynkellos*, is attested on a seal bearing the inscription, Σάβας μοναχὸς καὶ πρῶτος τῶν συγκέλλων, an honorific title which we can more easily imagine used in Constantinople than elsewhere. Michael Psellos, for instance, corresponded with a certain Leo Paraspondylos, whom he addresses as *protosynkellos*, but elsewhere he uses the title without a name and may have intended some other correspondent.[75] Of these three, the Vatopedi *higoumenos* fulfills the function of abbot that the poem alludes to, the *grammatikos* at Iviron is a promising candidate because of his level of culture, while the *protosynkellos* with the seal of the Theotokos belongs to the right Constantinopolitan milieu where one tends to place the origin of Clarke 15. De-

---

74. See Michael Jeffreys et al., *Prosopography of the Byzantine World*, 2016 ed. (London, 2017): "Sabas, grammatikos and monk at Iveron" (= Sabas 102), http://db.pbw.kcl.ac.uk/pbw2011/entity/person/108230; "Sabas, hegoumenos of Vatopedi on Athos" (= Sabas 107), http://db.pbw.kcl.ac.uk/pbw2011/entity/person/157402; and "Sabas, monk and protosynkellos" (= Sabas 20103 and boulloterion 6049), http://db.pbw.kcl.ac.uk/pbw2011/entity/boulloterion/6049.

75. Jeffreys and Lauxtermann, *Letters*, 429: although without a named addressee, "Most commentators also link M 6, P 1, and S 9 to the same addressee [Leon], not the only *protosynkellos* to whom Psellos writes, but the only one for whom that title seems so dominant a feature of his identification as to form an independent address."

Barbara Crostini

spite these enticing attestations, there is no guarantee of an identification.

Two more Sabas attestations in manuscripts from this period need to be considered. The first, mentioned by Lauxtermann himself, but only to be dismissed by him as "purely coincidental,"[76] occurs in an illustrated psalter: Mt. Athos, Dionysiou Monastery, MS 65, which bears a resemblance to Clarke 15 with respect to the learned verse inscriptions by Nikephoros Ouranos that complement the biblical text. While Rainer Stichel dated the manuscript according to its Easter tables to the fourteenth century,[77] current opinion has dated its origin to ca. 1100. Based on examination of the rare colour reproductions available,[78] the earlier dating is likely to be correct, a matter not without consequence for the highly charged theological imagery concerning the fate of the soul at death that prefaces the book.[79] The question really is what Sabas had to do with it, because, while Lauxtermann affirms that the manuscript "was produced on behalf of a monk called Sabas," Parpulov merely states parenthetically that the name of Sabas is found in the acrostic of a poem in the calendar of saints.[80] A more thorough investigation of the manuscript in connection to Clarke 15

---

76. Lauxtermann, "Perils," 199n22.
77. Rainer Stichel, *Studien zum Verhältnis von Text und Bild spät- und nachbyzantinischer Vergänglichkeitsdarstellungen* (Vienna, 1971), 70.
78. Parpulov, *Toward a History*, fig. 13. Parpulov dates this manuscript to the beginning of the twelfth century.
79. Stichel, *Studien*, 70–75 and figs. 7–9. Some relevant considerations are now found in Vasileios Marinis, *Death and the Afterlife in Byzantium: The Fate of the Soul in Theology, Liturgy, and Art* (Cambridge, 2017), 62–63 and fig. 11. Marinis publishes fol. 12r in colour and attributes the manuscript to the eleventh century.
80. Parpulov, *Toward a History*, 62 ("One Sabbas contrived to transform it into a special hymnographic canon.") and n66 for the acrostic that provides other names for Sabbas, characterized as "blind," and the witness of another codex to the poetic composition: Mt. Sinai, Monastery of Saint Catherine, MS gr. 1275, s.xiii, fols. 78r–94v.

may be extremely useful, even though the texts cited by Parpulov from Dionysiou 65 are different from those contained in the Oxford codex.

The second attestation has not found its way into the prosopographical record, though this Sabas was one of the main actors in a full-page miniature of the famous deluxe codex, Paris, Bibliothèque nationale de France, MS Coislin 79. This monk named Sabas in the inscription is depicted standing, in the act of reading from a lectern the very book of homilies of John Chrysostom contained in the book itself. His audience is none other than the Byzantine emperor. The latter is also depicted in another prefatory miniature of this manuscript surrounded by his court, consisting of four eunuchs. Sabas himself is portrayed as beardless, which may also group him in such a category.[81] There has been some debate as to the identification of the emperor in these portraits, and the hypothesis put forward by Ioannis Spatharakis,[82] and supported by later scholarship, is that the original imperial portrait of Michael IV Paphlagon was overpainted and the miniatures changed to match his successor, Nikephoros III Botaneiates. The overpainting represents a deliberate attempt at adapting the book to changing political circumstances. This interpretation has been recently challenged by Karin Krause, who dates the manuscript to 1078–1081, and who advocates the simpler explanation that any sign of tampering with these images is due to later attempts at restoration. The book and its minia-

---

81. On Sabas as a eunuch, see C. L. Dumitrescu, "Remarques en marge du Coislin 79: Les trois eunuques et le problème du donateur," *Byzantion* 57 (1987): 32–45 at 38. On monasteries of eunuchs in the eleventh century, see Shaun Tougher, "'The Angelic Life': Monasteries for Eunuchs," in *Byzantine Style, Religion and Civilization: In Honour of Sir Steven Runciman*, ed. Elizabeth M. Jeffreys (Cambridge, 2006), 238–52.

82. Ioannis Spatharakis, *The Portrait in Byzantine Illuminated Manuscripts* (Leiden, 1976), 107–18 and figs. 69–76.

Barbara Crostini

tures were always meant to have been made for, and be depictions of, Nikephoros.[83]

This dating and context fit so well with Clarke 15, that it is just possible to glimpse in this image of monk Sabas someone quite close to the charismatic spiritual leader mentioned in "Mark's" heartfelt prayer. The question of the identity and role of the Coislin Sabas, however, is not altogether solved by a simpler hypothesis about the manuscript's imperial portrait. Dumitrescu advances the possibility that the portrait of Sabas closely matches the features of one of the courtiers in the other full-page miniature, and tentatively suggests (though in the end rejecting) a possible identity between Sabas and the sponsor for this manuscript, John Metropolitan of Side, who was at one time (1071) also the *protoproedros* of the *protosynkelloi*. Although it is not the place here to review this case, the textual, visual, and prosopographical evidence could certainly benefit from being further/better contextualized.

In conclusion, a larger context for spiritual as opposed to practical travel seems more appropriate for the interpretation of the making of Clarke 15, a precious codex not only for the gold lettering of its epigrams and its decoration, but especially for the wealth of purpose-made verse compositions in high poetic style that mark it, as both Lauxtermann and Stefec have independently affirmed, as a product linked with the highest echelons of Byzantine courtiers. Parpulov has noted that the first text in this manuscript features an abbreviated version of Psellos's verses on the Psalter, which someone has taken the liberty of shortening and altering

---

83. Karin Krause, *Die illustrierten Homilien des Johannes Chrysostomos in Byzanz* (Wiesbaden, 2004), 183: "Es gibt keinen zwingenden Grund in Frage zu stellen, daß der Cod. Coislin. 79 mit seinen Frontispizzillustrationen speziell für Nikephoros III. angefertigt worden ist. Als Entstehungszeit des Manuskriptes ergeben sich folglich die Jahre 1078–1081."

even while the author of this text was still alive.[84] Indeed, Lauxtermann agrees that "the Bodleian manuscript ... was produced when Psellos was still alive," arguing that its readings, unfortunately unknown to Westerink, the first editor of these poems, are the best ones preserved in the tradition of this text.[85] Intriguingly too, one branch of the direct tradition of the paraphrase to the titles of the Psalms written in the margins of Clarke 15 attributes this composition to Psellos, whereas the other branch keeps it under the otherwise unknown authorship of Mark.[86]

Lauxtermann's philological conclusion that Clarke 15 is "not the archetype ... but an apograph of the master's copy"[87] is key to establish the closest possible link between this book and the author of these verses. The fact that Psellos also authored another paraphrasis of the titles that is more exegetical in tone need not, in itself, be an obstacle to considering this more scholastic version also as his.[88] It would repay further philological investigation into these texts to see whether Psellos's elusive authorship could be more clearly detected. This book could then be considered as marking his second and more definitive retreat into monastic seclusion with the name of Mark.

---

84. Parpulov, *Toward a History*, 130: "Even during the latter's [i.e., Psellos's] lifetime, his longish poem was cut down to size and used in abridged form."
85. Lauxtermann, "Perils," 197.
86. Ciccolella, "Carmi," 55 and n5. On the double transmission, see also Lauxtermann, "Perils," 198–99 and appendix 2 at 205–6, calling the Psellan branch "Ps.-Psellos."
87. Lauxtermann, "Perils," 199.
88. Ciccolella, "Carmi," 50, implicitly dismisses Mark's verses as an inferior composition: "... mentre il carme di Psello ha carattere esegetico, Marco monaco si è limitato a redigere per ogni salmo un titoletto più o meno appropriato."

Barbara Crostini

Towards a Function for Diminutive Manuscripts

I have argued in this paper against Lauxtermann's traveling hypothesis for a specific diminutive psalter, Clarke 15, on the basis of its size and an interpretation of its texts. While this negative revision applies specifically to the manuscript in question, the alternative proposal of a celebratory function of such small psalter books as gifts on the occasion of monastic profession is more generally put forward here.[89] This function would suitably harmonize the individual character that has been stressed in these eleventh-century psalters—whether or not a name is available besides the features pointing to intimacy—with the standard elements that are found interchangeably between different copies. Among such standard features, a set of Easter tables often provides the basis on which these psalters are dated. Nonetheless, the observation that no two tables are identical in years begun or span of years provided contributes another element to person- or event-specific individuation. The first date commemorated is likely to indicate a significant occasion, a moment in the life of the possessor, such as that of monastic profession. Variation in the span of years contemplated in these tables could perhaps be calculated according to the age of the receiver of the gift, reflecting the different stages of existence in which individuals joined monasteries. Such calendars could thus fulfill a practical purpose in the liturgical regulation of the individual monk, as well as contain an element of prediction or well-wishing divination as is sometimes found in other as-

---

89. On books as gifts, see Anthony Cutler, "Gifts and Gift Exchange as Aspects of the Byzantine, Arab and Related Economies," *Dumbarton Oaks Papers* 55 (2001): 247–78; John Lowden, "The Luxury Book as Diplomatic Gift," in *Byzantine Diplomacy: Papers from the Twenty-Fourth Spring Symposium of Byzantine Studies, Cambridge, March 1990*, ed. Jonathan Shepard and Simon Franklin (Aldershot, UK, 1990), 249–60.

pects of such psalters.[90] This scenario would fit a real-life situation better than that of acquiring a precious manuscript, burdened by additional pages of calendrical computus, for a trip. Finally, the imagery chosen for these psalters is explicitly eschatological, as in the unique miniatures of Dionysiou 65. Their focus on the fate of the soul of the individual monk enhances the likelihood that these personal books had a specific function to perform in the monastery as legacy and memento of a member whose soul was entrusted to the prayers of the community.

Weyl Carr provides some evidence for diminutive manuscripts belonging to monks, such as the twelfth-century St. Catherine's Monastery gr. 65, or the ninth-century Laurenziana, Conv. soppr. 36, "made by a monk for another monk."[91] However, for the most part, we have no firm indication for a monastic context. Nevertheless, in the context of monastic life, such a book could legitimately remain a prized possession of the newly professed, as entrance into the monastery often (though not always) entailed the abdication of worldly riches, to which a book, and especially one with sacred content, could be made an exception. The deluxe quality and high expenditure for these precious miniature psalters[92] could be the only sign of a former worldly status that the newly professed could be allowed to bring with him into the monastic enclosure.[93] At his death, the

---

90. Parpulov, "Psalters and Personal Piety," 88n47, indicates that the earliest example is Paris, Bibliothèque nationale de France, MS gr. 164. I have been unable to consult the article by Paul Canart referenced by Parpulov.

91. Weyl Carr, "Diminutive Byzantine Manuscripts," 150 and 149 respectively.

92. This element of tension between the book's precious value and its high spiritual content is explicitly dealt with in the self-referential verses in Clarke 15: see Stefec, "Anmerkungen," 345–46; Lauxtermann, "Perils," 200.

93. Inclusive language could appropriately be used here.

Barbara Crostini

book would naturally find a home in the monastery's library, or it could be sold for a good profit.[94]

That small psalters were gifts does not preclude the fact that they *could* travel. A particular example of mobility is represented by the eleventh-century Vienna, Nationalbibliothek, MS theol. gr. 336, another Greek miniature psalter (100 x 80 mm.) made "for someone associated with St. Gereon, Cologne, in 1077."[95] Since this German foundation is dated 1069, one could imagine among its recruits a monk of Eastern provenance, who arrived bearing a profession gift.[96] Surely such international exchanges of 'wandering' monks were more common than we tend to envisage. One example is the journey of St. Symeon from the Holy Land to Trier,

---

94. Weyl Carr's diminutive manuscripts also include a list of gospels, for which these arguments would not be unfitting. However, I have restricted my discussion here to psalters.

95. Weyl Carr, "Diminutive Byzantine Manuscripts," 136. Colour images of this manuscript are still not available. It is undergoing conservation and could not be seen on my recent trip to the National Library in Vienna (April 2017). Reference still needs to be made to the rare and dated publication of Paul Buberl and Hans Gerstinger, *Die byzantinischen Handschriften*, vol. 2, *Die Handschriften des X.–XVIII. Jahrhunderts*, Die illuminierten Handschriften und Inkunabeln der Nationalbibliothek in Wien, 4, Beschreibendes Verzeichnis der illuminierten Handschriften in Österreich, 8.4 (Leipzig, 1938), 35, associating it closely to Clarke 15 and Athos Vatopedi 761.

96. Ernst Gamillscheg, "Beobachtungen zum Oeuvre des Kopisten Michael Panerges," *Chrisograf* 3 (2009): 76–93 at 92, offers the different explanation that this manuscript was a diplomatic gift. Although size and function cannot be paired as a matter of course, I still prefer to consider as "diplomatic gifts" between rulers or at the higher levels in the ecclesiastical hierarchy manuscripts of more considerable size and value. See in addition E. Dobrynina, ed., *Deâniâ i poslaniâ apostolov Greceskaâ illûuminovannaâ rukopis' 1072 g. iz sobraniia naoutchnoü biblioteki Moskousko vo ouniversitetasbornik statej = The Greek Illuminated Praxapostolos Dated 1072 in the Scientific Library of Moscow State University: Collected Articles* (Moscow, 2004), which was recommended to me by the anonymous reviewer of this paper, but which I was unable to consult.

where his Easter ascetic lifestyle attracted attention: some parchment manuscripts that include a *Prophetologion*, apparently enabling the continued recitation of the liturgy in Greek in his new German setting, were displayed together with his relics.[97]

Such journeys must have been especially frequent between Byzantium and Palestine. Although these exchanges do not explain *how* or precisely *where* these manuscripts were made, for example in the case of the twins Vat. gr. 342 (Constantinople) and Add. 36928 (Palestine), they could go some way to explaining *why* some codices were made to resemble each other. A monk would be eager to take with him a token mirroring a more famous Byzantine artefact as a remembrance of his origins, or be keen to carry and eventually leave behind a sign that displayed and stood for his cultural ideals.

In the case of Clarke 15, a monastic connection is explicitly established by the initial verses, spoken in the first person by Mark the Monk. According to Lauxtermann, Mark is the patron behind this small expensive book and at the same time its recipient. Unlike most other patrons, Mark has contributed his own poetic compositions to the making of this psalter. In these poems, Mark is alluding to his own story behind joining the monastery. The troubles Lauxtermann sensitively highlights are best described as existential, embracing both a spiritual and a practical dimension, but have, I would argue, nothing to do with physical journeying. Rather, the redemptive path described, not without dramatic turns, is that of a return to monastic life, a second profession marked by this expensive and elaborate gift.

---

97. Sysse G. Engberg, "Trier and Sinai: Saint Symeon's Book," *Scriptorium* 59 (2005): 132–46.

Barbara Crostini

The year of this manuscript's making, 1078, indeed coincided with the year of Psellos's death,[98] and a typical deathbed conversion would be in character with this man's life and times, when entering a monastery at the last hour was not uncommon. Psellos had only to choose what house might take him from among the many he had been patron over in his lifetime.[99] It is difficult to rein in the feeling that, if the author of Clarke's verses was alive, he was also very probably not too far from the milieu of production of this manuscript, that of the literary active and bitterly factional circles of Constantinople's eleventh-century court.[100]

Uppsala University

---

98. See Jeffreys and Lauxtermann, *Letters*, 3 (thus, closing a long debate over the date of his death).

99. Ibid., 42–58.

100. The hypothesis advanced by E. A. Fisher, "Nicomedia or Galatia? Where was Psellos' Church of the Archangel Michael?," in *GONIMOS: Neoplatonic and Byzantine Studies Presented to Leendert G. Westerink at 75*, ed., John Duffy and John Peradotto (Buffalo, NY, 1988), 175–87 at 77, that Psellos retreated to the monastery at Sykeon, as celebrated in his *Or. Hag.* 5, could in fact open an alternative scenario for the production and reception of this psalter in the heart of Anatolia, but in any case not too far from Constantinople.

Behind the Scenes: Establishing a Scriptorium in the Eleventh-Century Monastery of Saint-Sépulcre, Cambrai

Tjamke Snijders

THE monastery of Saint-Sépulcre, located in the city of Cambrai in northern France, was founded in 1064. Its first generation of monks included a man who called himself Fulbert the Sinner, "Fulbertus Peccator." He was a seasoned scribe who oversaw the establishment of Saint-Sépulcre's scriptorium. He was also a proud man, who left his "signature" by means of a colophon in several manuscripts on which he

* This article was written at KU Leuven, KU Leuven Libraries, Special Collections, Mgr. Ladeuzestraat 21, B-3000 Leuven, Belgium; and at Ghent University with the support of the Research Foundation-Flanders (FWO).

Abstract: Little work has thoroughly examined the problems that faced startup scriptoria in the High Middle Ages. This article examines the scriptorium of Saint-Sépulcre in the first decades after this Cambrai monastery was founded in 1064. A man who called himself Fulbertus Peccator ("Fulbert the Sinner") led the scriptorium during those years. He wrote at least 1,100 folios of foundational texts, but could not single-handedly fill the entire library. Fulbert therefore encouraged most, if not all, of Saint-Sépulcre's monks to participate in the production of hagiographical manuscripts, even if those monks were wholly unqualified. This article demonstrates that Fulbert's unusual decision not only helped fill the library with the hagiographical texts it needed, but also changed the significance of the resulting manuscripts for the monastic community. Much more than the sum of their parts, these manuscripts were created as objects that represented the communal spirit and the vibrancy of the newly founded monastery of Saint-Sépulcre.

Keywords: Fulbertus Peccator, Fulbert the Sinner, Cambrai, Saint-Sépulcre, Scriptoria, Hagiography, Paleography.

worked.[1] This habit allows us to reconstruct his scribal output and to analyze many decisions that were made in Saint-Sépulcre's fledgling scriptorium: which texts were copied and which were ignored, what kinds of manuscripts were delegated to relatively untrained scribes, and which organizational principles were adhered to. Fulbert's colophons reveal how he established and organized a scriptorium in Saint-Sépulcre.

The presence of these colophons also allows us to understand how these manuscripts acquired symbolic meaning at their moment of production. Of course, manuscripts had meaning because they were gathering places for texts, and these texts were meaningful in and of themselves. However, manuscripts also acquired meaning because, as objects, they embodied the creativity, the skill, and the associational value of the scribe(s) and/or illuminator(s) who worked on them.[2] A text that was physically written by the abbot of a monastery surely had a different meaning for the community than a text that was laboriously copied out by a young novice, not because the words were different, but because the text embodied some of the status and skills of its scribe. Put differently, manuscripts acquired symbolic significance partly from the circumstances and the people that produced them. This article shows how Fulbert's organization of a new scriptorium influenced the significance of the manuscripts that were created there.

---

1. The most recent study of Saint-Sépulcre's scriptorium is Denis Muzerelle, *Manuscrits datés des bibliothèques de France*, vol. 1, *Cambrai* (Paris, 2000), xxii–xxv. On the colophons of Fulbert, see Bénédictins du Bouveret, *Colophons de manuscrits occidentaux des origines au XVIe siècle* (Fribourg, 1965–82), 2:133, nos. 4607–4609.

2. Karen L. Jolly, "Dismembering and Reconstructing Ms Durham, Cathedral Library, A.IV.19," in *Scraped, Stroked, and Bound: Materially Engaged Readings of Medieval Manuscripts*, ed. Jonathan Wilcox (Turnhout, 2013), 177–200 at 198–99.

Behind the Scenes

FULBERT THE SINNER

The early history of Saint-Sépulcre has never been the subject of much research.[3] According to one eighteenth-century manuscript, its foundations were laid in 1047, when an epidemic swept through Cambrai and there were just too many bodies to bury.[4] Bishop Gerard I founded a small church near the city walls to bury the poor and the strangers in the name of the Holy Sepulchre. In 1064 his successor Lietbertus constructed a monastery next to the church, dedicating it to Christ and his Holy Sepulchre, his Holy Mother, and all God's Saints, and assigned an abbot and some monks to the new location. A bright light appeared in the heavens, and twenty-two bodies of saints were gathered to celebrate the foundation of Saint-Sépulcre.[5]

---

3. Notwithstanding, there are no fewer than 1,421 (mostly) unstudied documents from Saint-Sépulcre's archives awaiting their historian in the Archives départementales du Nord in Lille, France (série 3H). Even though most materials postdate the thirteenth century, there are some eleventh-and twelfth century items of interest, including 3H2/5 (the oldest pontifical privileges); 3H56 (donations); 3H73 (local conflict); 3H188, 200, and 209 (property); 3H255–3H257 (sixteenth-century cartularies); 3H262 (a nineteenth-century copy of the *Chronologia stemmatica*).

4. *Chronologia stemmatica beati fundatoris et abbatum ecclesiae ac monasterii Sancti Sepulchri Cameracensis, ordinis Sancti Benedicti cum brevi expositione vitae, gestorum et praeminentiarum eorumdem ex actis authenticis in eodem monasterio asservatis collecta anno 1740*, in Douai, Bibliothèque Marceline Desbordes-Valmore, MS 899. A virulent epidemic indeed decimated Flanders in 1046 and Hainaut in 1056 according to Lodewyk Torfs, *Fastes des calamités publiques survenues dans les Pays-Bas et particulièrement en Belgique, depuis les temps les plus reculés jusqu'à nos jours* (Paris and Tournai, 1859), 17.

5. See also Alphonse Wauters et al., eds., *Table chronologique des chartes et diplômes imprimés concernant l'histoire de la Belgique*, 11 vols. (Brussels, 1866–1912) 1:515; *Diplomata belgica: Les sources diplomatiques des Pays-Bas méridionaux au Moyen Âge = The Diplomatic Sources from the Medieval Southern Low Countries*, no. 3824, http://www.diplomata-belgica.be/charter_details_fr.php?dibe_id=3824.

Tjamke Snijders

At the time of the monastery's foundation, the diocese of Cambrai was under intense pressure. Cambrai was subservient to the Holy Roman Empire in worldly matters and adhered to the Pope in spiritual matters. This duality became problematic when in 1056 the six-year-old Henry IV was elected King of the Romans and the ensuing political struggles between the Empire and the Pope profoundly affected Cambrai. Around 1093 the diocese was split into one part that shed its imperial connections (Arras) and another that maintained its attachment to the Empire (and retained the name of Cambrai).[6] These tensions forced newly founded Saint-Sépulcre to tread carefully regarding the religious and political statements it made.

For the first decades of its existence, Saint-Sépulcre was a small and relatively poor abbey. Bishop Lietbertus tried to look out for his foundation, providing it with the relics of local saints as well as with goods and privileges.[7] In 1075 he asked Pope Gregory VII to take the abbey under his protec-

---

6. Bernard Delmaire, *Le diocèse d'Arras de 1093 au milieu du XIVe siècle: Recherches sur la vie religieuse dans le nord de la France au Moyen Âge* (Arras, 1994), 163–64, 203–4, 402; Maurice Chartier, "Cambrai (diocèse)," in *Dictionnaire d'histoire et de géographie ecclésiastique*, ed. Alfred Baudrillart et al., 32 vols. to date (Paris, 1912–), 11:547–65; Irven M. Resnick, "Odo of Cambrai and the Investiture Crisis in the Early Twelfth Century," *Viator* 28 (1997): 83–98; and John S. Ott, *Bishops, Authority, and Community in Northwestern Europe, c. 1050–1150*, Cambridge Studies in Medieval Life and Thought, 4th ser., 102 (Cambridge, 2015), 197–221 ("Sanctity and History in a Border Diocese: The *Vita* of Lietbert of Cambrai [1051–76]").

7. For the early history of Saint-Sépulcre, see Rudolf of Saint-Sépulcre, "Vita Lietberti episcopi Cameracensis auctore Rudulfo monacho S. Sepulchri Cameracensis," ed. Adolphus Hofmeister, in *Monumenta Germaniae historica ... Scriptores*, vol. 30.2 (Leipzig, 1934), 838–68 at 859–61 and 866–68; "Gesta episcoporum Cameracensium," ed. Lud. C. Bethmann, in *Monumenta Germaniae historica ... Scriptores*, vol. 7, ed. Georg Heinrich Pertz (Hannover, 1846; repr. Leipzig, 1925), 402–525 at 496–97; and the *Chronologia stemmatica*.

tion.[8] One year later, Bishop Lietbertus was succeeded by Gerard II (1076–92) who confirmed his predecessor's donations to "Abbot Walter and the ten poor monks" who lived in Saint-Sépulcre in 1079.[9] Contemporary historical sources do not pay Saint-Sépulcre much notice.[10] The monastery was obviously struggling.

Nevertheless, Saint-Sépulcre diverted very significant resources into manuscript production. No less than thirteen manuscripts have been preserved from the period between 1076 and 1092, and the monks likely produced many more. Five of these manuscripts were signed with the vainly modest phrase "I entreat everyone who reads this to remember Fulbert the Sinner (and Scribe)." The phrasing varies slightly from manuscript to manuscript, but the scribe always identified himself as "Fulbertus Peccator."[11] Seven more unsigned manuscripts also contain fragments of texts that were written by Fulbert, who was thus actively involved in twelve of the thirteen manuscripts preserved from this

---

8. Lille, Archives départementales du Nord, 3H2/5, edited in *Quellen und Forschungen zum Urkunden- und Kanzleiwesen Papst Gregors VII*, ed. Leo Santifaller, Studi e testi 190 (Vatican City, 1957), 86–88.

9. *Notitia ecclesiarum Belgii*, ed. Aubert le Mire (Antwerp, 1630), 206; see also Erik Van Mingroot, "Gérard II de Lessines," in *Dictionnaire d'histoire et de géographie ecclésiastique*, 20:751–55.

10. See, for example, Raoul de Saint-Trond, *Gesta abbatum Trudonensium I–VII*, ed. Paul Tombeur, Corpus christianorum, Continuatio mediaevalis 257 (Turnhout, 2013); Steven Vanderputten, "Compilation et réinvention à la fin du douzième siècle: Andre de Marchiennes, le *Chronicon Marchianense* et l'histoire primitive d'une abbaye bénédictine (édition et critique des sources)," *Sacris erudiri* 42 (2003): 403–36; Folcuin, "Gesta abbatum Lobiensium," in *Monumenta Germaniae historica ... Scriptores*, vol. 7, 52–74, and Folcuin, "Gesta abbatum Sithiensium," ed. O. Holder-Egger, in *Monumenta Germaniae historica ... Scriptores*, vol. 13 (Hannover, 1881; repr. Leipzig, 1925), 607–35; and the *Gesta episcoporum Cameracensium*.

11. Muzerelle, *Manuscrits datés ... Cambrai*, xxii. See Cambrai, Bibliothèque municipale (also known as the Médiathèque d'agglomération de Cambrai), MSS 215, 217, 218, 247, and 819.

period.[12] One of these has been dated with relative accuracy. Cambrai, Bibliothèque municipale, MS 864, fol. 125v contains a list of the bishops of Cambrai that was continued in the original hand up to Bishop Gerard II (1076–92).[13] This list thus places the production of Cambrai 864 in the years between 1076 and 1092 and by extension dates all thirteen manuscripts to that approximate period.

Who was this Fulbert the Sinner? As already indicated, he appears to have possessed a strong sense of his own importance, seeing fit to leave his name on several of the manuscripts he produced.[14] He put his name in very conspicuous places, such as the title page of Cambrai 215, where he signed his name in bold red ink (fol. 1r):

PRIMA PARS IN IOB
Liber sancti Sepulchri Cameracensis.
Si quis abstulerit, anathema sit.
Servanti benedictio, tollenti maledictio.
Amen, amen, amen, amen.
Obsecro quicumque hęc legeris, ut Fulberti scriptoris et peccatoris memineris.

Denis Muzerelle speculates that Fulbert may have been a lay scribe because he refers to himself as *scriptor* and *peccator*, but never as *frater, monachus, diaconus,* or *presbyter*. On the other hand, Muzerelle also notes that the "Fulbertus c[onversus] et mo[nachus]" who is inscribed in

---

12. Cambrai, Bibliothèque municipale, MSS 216, 219, 504, 807, 846, 863, and 864. Cambrai, Bibliothèque municipale, MS 506 does not contain interventions by Fulbert, but several of the hands from Cambrai 846, 863, and 864 are present, thus dating it to roughly the same period.

13. Muzerelle, *Manuscrits datés … Cambrai*, 102–3.

14. Richard Gameson, "'Signed' Manuscripts from Early Romanesque Flanders: Saint-Bertin and Saint-Vaast," in *Pen in Hand: Medieval Scribal Portraits, Colophons and Tools,* ed. Michael Gullick (Walkern, UK, 2006), 31–73 at 31.

Behind the Scenes

Saint-Sépulcre's *necrologium* on December 31 could well be Fulbert the Sinner.[15] Lay or monk, Fulbert was not shy about signing his name, and he remained the only person to do so in the scriptorium of Saint-Sépulcre for at least a century.[16] He was without any doubt the monastery's most important scribe and saw himself as a person whose name was worthy to be remembered in a manuscript context.

There may be an indication of Fulbert's identity in the opening lines of the *Vita secunda Aichardi* in Cambrai 864. Saint Aichardus (also called Aychadrus) was one of the founding abbots of the Abbey of Jumièges in the late seventh century. In the ninth century a monk from Jumièges first wrote the *Vita prima Aichardi*, which was rewritten later in the tenth or eleventh century as the *Vita secunda Aichardi* with the avowed purpose of improving its inane style.[17] The rewriter begins his work with the words "I, Fulbert the Sinner, salute the gentlemen of the monastery of Jumièges, that is to say, its most holy brothers" (*Dominis suis Gimmetiensis coenobii scilicet fratribus sanctissimis, Fulbertus Peccator salutem*). In most manuscripts, this salutation is removed because it was neither written by a famous author nor relevant to the contents of the *Vita*, but the Saint-Sépulcre scribe conscientiously copied it out and even colored the name of "Fulbertus Peccator" with red ink to underline its importance.[18] Could it be that the Fulbert

---

15. Muzerelle, *Manuscrits datés ... Cambrai*, xxii–iii.

16. An exception to this is a certain Lanvinus, who wrote Cambrai, Bibliothèque municipale, MS 544. See Muzerelle, *Manuscrits datés ... Cambrai*, xxiii.

17. *Bibliotheca hagiographica latina* [hereafter cited as *BHL*], Subsidia hagiographica 6 (Bruxelles, 1898–99; repr. 1992), 30–31, nos. 181 and 182 respectively.

18. Valenciennes, Bibliothèque municipale, MS 514, fol. 78r (Saint-Amand-les-Eaux, ca. 1165), and Douai, Bibliothèque Marceline Desbordes-Valmore, MSS 867, fol. 49r (Marchiennes, ca. 1050–75), and 836, fol. 179r (Marchiennes, ca. 1175–1200).

the Sinner who rewrote the Life of Abbot Aichardus was the same man who led the scriptorium of Saint-Sépulcre? Unfortunately, the identity of Fulbert the Author is uncertain, and even the century in which he worked is open to debate. Felice Lifshitz and John Howe have argued that the *terminus post quem* for the *Vita secunda* is the reign of Abbot Anno of Jumièges (940/42–973). During his abbacy, the monks of Jumièges produced a luxurious manuscript about Saint Aichardus that still featured the *Vita prima*, which indicates that the *Vita secunda* had not yet been written.[19] The *terminus ante quem* for the *Vita secunda* is provided by the three earliest surviving manuscripts: Rouen, Bibliothèque municipale, MS 1409 (Y.189) from Jumièges (which Lifshitz thought was produced shortly before 1037, but has been more convincingly dated to ca. 1078–95 and is written in a hand similar to that of Cambrai 864);[20] Oxford, Bodleian Library, MS Bodley 852 (2611), which Howe places in Jumièges and dates to the 1070s;[21] and Cambrai 864 (1076–92). The *Vita secunda Aichardi* must thus have been produced between 940/42 at the earliest, and the 1070s at the latest.

Judging from the preserved codices, the *Vita prima Aichardi* was popular from the tenth century until sometime

---

19. John Howe, "The Hagiography of Jumièges (Province of Haute-Normandie)," in *L'hagiographie du haut moyen âge en Gaule du Nord: Manuscrits, textes et centres de production*, ed. Martin Heinzelmann (Stuttgart, 2001), 91–126 at 106; Felice Lifschitz, *The Norman Conquest of Pious Neustria: Historiographic Discourse and Saintly Relics, 684–1090* (Toronto, 1995), 123, and 134n87.

20. Howe, "Hagiography of Jumièges," 101–2; Monique-Cécile Garand, Geneviève Grand, and Denis Muzerelle, *Ouest de la France et pays de Loire*, vol. 7 of *Catalogue des manuscrits en écriture latine portant des indications de date, de lieu ou de copiste*, ed. Charles Samaran and Robert Marical, 2 vols. (Paris, 1984), 1:331 and pl. 27.

21. Howe, "Hagiography of Jumièges," 102.

between 1024 and 1039,[22] whereupon no more copies were made of that text for at least thirty years. This marked falling off in production fits with Fulbert's claim that the *Vita prima* became obsolete. A handful of manuscripts containing Fulbert's *Vita secunda* survive from the 1070s onward,[23] which indicates that he wrote his *Vita secunda* in the lull between ca. 1024 and the 1070s.

Fulbert the Author also rewrote a Life of Saint Romain (*Vita tertia Romani*) for the brothers of Rouen, beginning his work in a very similar way: "Dominis et confratribus suis sancte Rothomagensis ecclesie matris filiis, Fulbertus Peccator salutem."[24] Again, Lifshitz places its moment of production fairly early, between 919 and 960, whereas Le Maho suspects that the text was produced after the *translatio* of Saint Romain in 1032.[25] Nancy Gauthier thinks that the text was written around 1056[26] and Constable places it in the late eleventh century.[27] In any case, the oldest known manuscript (the so-called *Livre d'ivoire*) with this Life of

---

22. *BHL*, 1061, no. 7312 in Paris, Bibliothèque nationale de France, MS lat. 1805 (s.x); and *BHL*, 30, no. 181 in Avranches, Bibliothèque municipale, MS 99 (s.x–s.xi), in Arras, Bibliothèque municipale, MS 1029 (s.xi$^{1/4}$ after 1006), in Boulogne-sur-mer, Bibliothèque municipale, MS 106 (probably copied from Arras 1029), and in Brussels, KBR, MS II 992 (ca. 1024/5–ca. 1035/9).

23. Rouen 1409 (Y.189) (ca. 1078–95); Bodley 852 (2611) (1070s); Cambrai 864 (1076–92); and Douai 867 (s.xi, prob. third quarter). The extensive dossier of Saint Romain has not yet been studied in enough detail to draw parallels.

24. *BHL*, 1061, no. 7313.

25. Jacques Le Maho, "La production éditoriale à Jumièges vers le milieu du Xe siècle," *Tabularia: Sources écrites des mondes normands médiévaux* 1 (2001): 11–32 at 31–32 and 32n78; Lifshitz, *Norman Conquest*, 178–79.

26. Nancy Gauthier, "Rouen pendant le Haut Moyen-Age (650–850)," in *La Neustrie: Les pays au nord de la Loire de 650 à 850*, ed. Hartmut Atsma, 2 vols. (Paris, 1989), 2:1–20 at 3n5.

27. Giles Constable, *The Reformation of the Twelfth Century* (Cambridge, 1996), 141.

Saint Romain was produced around 1070.[28] In short, the *Vita tertia Romani* must have been produced around 919 at the earliest, and around 1070 at the latest; but most likely between ca. 1032 and ca. 1070.

Fulbert was a common name.[29] Yet I am disinclined to assume the existence of two separate author-scribes who both called themselves "Fulbertus Peccator," had the unusual habit of signing their work, and flourished around the mid-eleventh century in northern France.[30] There probably was but one Fulbertus Peccator, whose familiarity with Aichardus of Jumièges and Romanus of Rouen suggests that he was educated in Normandy—perhaps in the cathedral of Rouen, the monastery of Saint-Ouen, Jumièges, or Saint-Wandrille.

The people of Cambrai's traditional interest in Saint Aichardus strengthens the hypothesis that there was one Fulbert the Sinner who spent his youth in Normandy before

---

28. Rouen, Bibliothèque municipale, MS 1405 (Y.27), also known as the *Livre d'ivoire* of Rouen cathedral, was not bound together to its present form until the thirteenth century. The manuscript originally contained a list of bishops from Rouen that ends with Maurillius (1055–67) and the *Acta archiepiscoporum Rotomagensium* in this manuscript has been dated ca. 1070; see Richard Allen, "The *Acta archiepiscoporum Rotomagensium*: Study and Edition," *Tabularia: Sources écrites des mondes normands médiévaux* 9 (2009): 1–66 at 5. The Life and Office of Saint Romain appear as part of that same section.

29. Muzerelle, *Manuscrits datés ... Cambrai*, xxiii; David S. Spear, "Les doyens du chapitre cathédral de Rouen, durant la période ducale," *Annales de Normandie* 33 (1983): 91–120; Spear, "Les archidiacres de Rouen au cours de la période ducale," *Annales de Normandie* 34 (1984): 15–50.

30. The idea that Fulbert rewrote the miracles of Saint Audomarus (*BHL*, 122, no. 760) between 1036/7 and 1092 has recently been discredited (Allen, "*Acta archiepiscoporum Rotomagensium*," 12). Fulbertus Peccator has on occasion been identified with archdeacon Fulbert of Rouen (ca. 1047–ca. 1075), who may or may not have been the same person as Fulbert "the Sophist" who was in Saint-Évroult with Bishop Maurilius in 1056. One or other of these Fulberti may also have written the *Acta archiepiscoporum Rotomagensium* around 1070.

Behind the Scenes

moving to Saint-Sépulcre. This interest went back to the ninth century when the Normans had assaulted Jumièges. The monks of Jumièges had fled their abbey, taking the relics of Aichardus with them.[31] They had taken refuge in the priory of Haspres, which was situated in the diocese of Cambrai only a few miles from the episcopal see. Even though Bishop Gerard I returned Aichardus's relics to Jumièges around 1038, the bishops of Cambrai continued to take an interest in Aichardus, Haspres, and Jumièges, and the Cambrai populace continued to venerate the saint.[32] At Saint-Sépulcre's foundation in 1064, Bishop Lietbertus acquired a relic of "Sanctus Aicadrus abbas et confessor a cenobio Hasprehiensi" for his new community.[33] Perhaps Fulbert was involved in this acquisition. We may suspect that he was a monk with an intimate knowledge of Saint Aichardus. Perhaps Bishop Lietbertus asked Fulbert to rewrite the old-fashioned Life of Aichardus when the relic

---

31. Jean Laporte, "La date de l'exode de Jumièges," in *Jumièges: Congrès scientifique du XIIIe centenaire, Rouen, 10–12 juin 1954*, 2 vols. (Rouen, 1955), 1:47–48 at 48.

32. Steven Vanderputten and Brigitte Meijns, "Realities of Reformist Leadership in Early Eleventh-Century Flanders: The Case of Leduin, Abbot of Saint-Vaast," *Traditio* 65 (2010): 47–74 at 57, 60–61. The name "Aichadre" figures in the 812 litany of Cambrai (Maurice Coens, "Anciennes litanies des saints," *Analecta bollandiana* 62 [1944]: 131–322 at 280) as well as in the litanies of several other monasteries in Cambrai, such as Marchiennes: "Aicadre" in Douai, Bibliothèque Marcelline Desbordes-Valmore, MS 68, fol. 8v, and "Aycadre" in Brussels, KBR, MS 14682 (see Coens, "Anciennes litanies," 278). Aichardus's life can be found in at least nine Cambrai manuscripts: KBR II 992 from Saint-Ghislain; Douai, Bibliothèque Marcelline Desbordes-Valmore, MSS 151, 836, and 867 from Marchiennes; Cambrai, Bibliothèque municipale, MS 864 from Saint-Sépulcre; Arras, Bibliothèque municipale, MSS 14, 573, and 1029 from Saint-Vaast; and Valenciennes, Bibliothèque municipale, MS 514 from Saint-Amand). See also Charles Mériaux, *Gallia irradiata: Saints et sanctuaires dans le nord de la Gaule du haut Moyen Âge* (Stuttgart, 2006), 283–84.

33. Rodulf of Saint-Sépulcre, "Vita Lietberti," 868.

was donated to Saint-Sépulcre, to re-ignite local interest for the saint.[34] Unfortunately, I have no way to confirm or disprove such speculations. It is likely, however, that Fulbert the Sinner's expertise regarding the *Vita Aichardi* made him a person of some authority in Saint-Sépulcre.

FULBERT AS "SCRIBE IN CHARGE"

In Saint-Sépulcre Fulbert functioned as the "scribe in charge" of the scriptorium.[35] He single-handedly effected copies of Smaragdus's commentary on the Rule of Benedict, known as *The Monk's Diadem,* a very popular sermon on ascetic life by Ephraim the Syrian,[36] Cassian's discussion of the rules and morality of monastic life and asceticism in the *Institutions* and *Conferences*,[37] as well as a five-volume copy of Gregory the Great's *Commentary in Job/Magna moralia*, which he left unfinished.[38] As Denis Muzerelle puts it, "one is probably able to say at which leaf [Fulbert] died," as his hand begins to decline steadily from the fourth volume onwards, becomes almost unrecognizable in the fifth, and stops forever on fol. 89r. In total, Fulbert copied more than 1,100 folios of works that were essential for the monks in newly-founded Saint-Sépulcre. Through his copying activities, Fulbert taught the community members how to live their lives as monks.

Fulbert was not particularly concerned about the stylistic homogeneity of the manuscripts he produced. His hand

---

34. Cf. Howe, "Hagiography of Jumièges," 125.
35. For the term "scribe in charge," see Francis Newton, *The Scriptorium and Library at Monte Cassino, 1058–1105*, Cambridge Studies in Palaeography and Codicology 7 (Cambridge, 1999), 136n79.
36. Cambrai 819: *Diadema monachorum* and *Liber de compunctione cordis* (also known as *Sermo asceticus*).
37. Cambrai 247, 504.
38. Cambrai 215, 216, 217, 218, and 219; Muzerelle, *Manuscrits datés … Cambrai*, xxiii.

varied quite significantly from manuscript to manuscript, which has led Muzerelle to remark that paleographers would probably not have tried to link all these manuscripts to the same person if Fulbert had not habitually left behind a colophon attesting to his work.[39] But apart from the changes in hand—which may have been the simple result of getting older—he also varied the material characteristics of his manuscripts.

The manuscripts Fulbert signed are all roughly equal in size, measuring between 230 x 170 mm. and 270 x 180 mm. (or 401–486 sq. cm.), and having 97 to 153 folios and 28 to 30 lines per page. The manuscripts that he co-wrote with other scribes in Saint-Sépulcre vary much more significantly, measuring between 190 x 120 mm. and 310 x 220 mm. (or 282–691 sq. cm.), and having 111 to 292 folios and 26 to 38 lines per page. The text block varies from 185 x 125 mm. (in Cambrai 215) to 250 x 180 mm. (Cambrai 807). In manuscripts that were written by multiple scribes, the text block is not even consistent within a manuscript: Cambrai 864, for example, has text blocks of 257 x 170 mm., 256 x 177 mm., and 242 x 181 mm. While Fulbert punctuates Cambrai 215 with a *media distinctio* and *punctus elevatus*, most of the other Saint-Sépulcre scribes use the older system of *subdistinctio*, *media distinctio*, and *distinctio*. Fulbert's average initial is three lines high, while his colleagues usually left space for lager initials: 4.18 lines in Cambrai 864 or 4.69 lines in Cambrai 863. These numbers indicate that Fulbert may not have valued a strictly homogeneous and identifiable style for himself, and certainly did not impose it on his subordinates.

Fulbert cooperated with other monks in four manuscripts, all of which are hagiographical.[40] Of the 820 folios containing saints' lives in these codices, he wrote one third

---

39. Muzerelle, *Manuscrits datés ... Cambrai*, xxii.
40. Cambrai 807, 846, 863, and 864.

(247 folios) by himself and left the rest to his monks. Fulbert started each codex with a *praescriptio*—he wrote the first couple of lines to set the size, spacing, and level of formality that was required in this manuscript and left his subordinates to finish the rest of the texts.[41] The *praescriptio* indicates that Fulbert may have used the hagiographical codices as projects to train his scribes. Was that indeed his intention, and if so, what may his educational goals have been?

CAMBRAI, BIBLIOTHÈQUE MUNICIPALE, MS 864

Cambrai 864 throws some light on Fulbert's intentions. The manuscript contains the lives and passions of thirty-nine saints. Fulbert wrote the first five folios in this manuscript.[42] The aspect of his script is small, regular, and rather square written at a very straight angle (figs. 1–3). Among the most notable features of his hand is the morphology of **g**, with a descender attached to the middle of the bowl and ending almost horizontally. He places **r** on the baseline, though long **s** descends slightly below the line and consists of three strokes. He makes distinct wedges on his ascenders (which are not always placed at the top of the ascender), long descenders of **x**, elongated caudatae consisting of two strokes in a **v**-formation, and very broad, rounded **ct**-ligatures.

The other hands in the codex are of varying quality. Some of the most practiced hands are situated at the beginning. They try to imitate Fulbert's morphology, though they never quite manage to capture the square regularity

---

41. Sidney Tibbetts, "*Praescriptiones,* Student Scribes and the Carolingian Scriptorium," in *La collaboration dans la production de l'écrit médiéval: Actes du XIIIe colloque du Comité international de paléographie latine (Weingarten, 22–25 septembre 2000),* ed. Herrad Spilling (Paris, 2003), 25–38 at 26–32.

42. For the identification of Fulbert's hand in this codex, see Muzerelle, *Manuscrits datés ... Cambrai,* 103.

Figure 1.

Characteristic Letterforms in the Hand of Fulbert the Sinner.
Cambrai, Bibliothèque municipale, MS 864,
fols. 23v, 24r, 125r (details).

g

r and long s

wedges on ascenders: **b**, **d**, and **l**

x

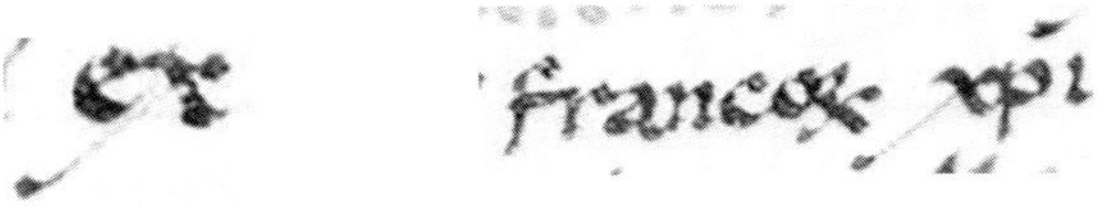

v-shaped caudata

ct-ligature

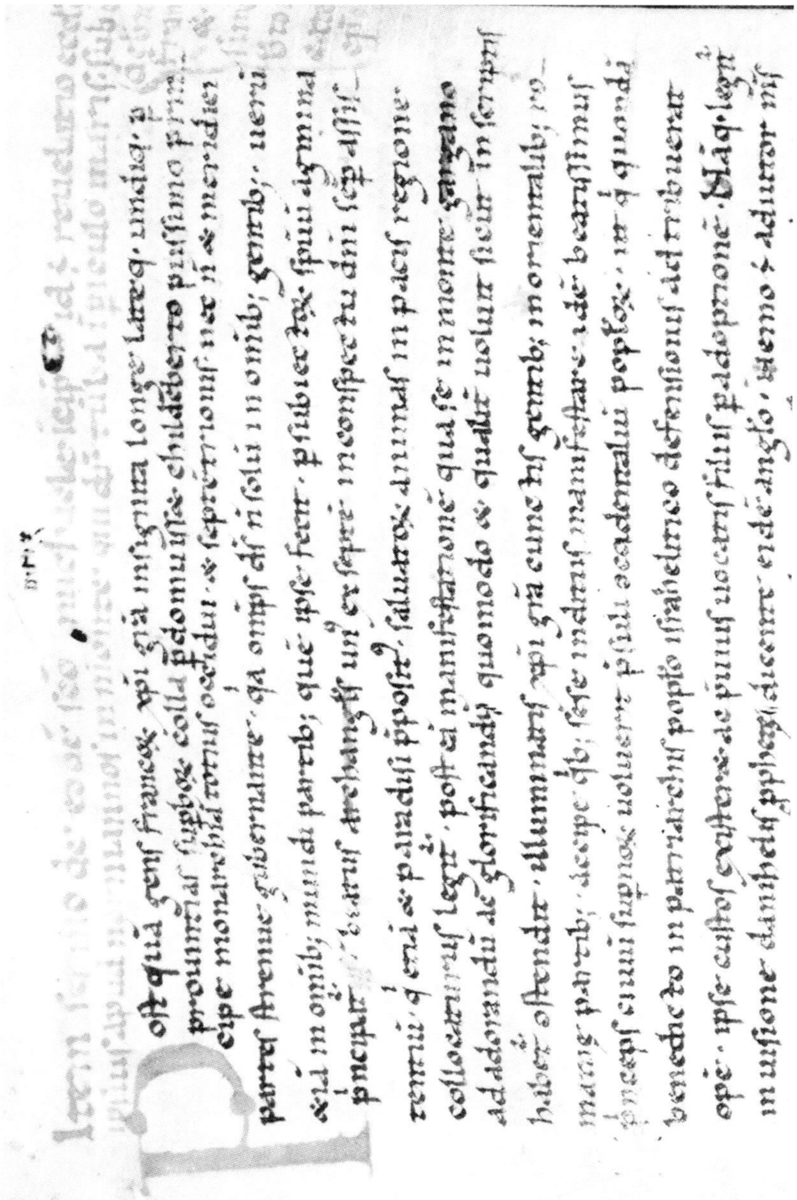

Figure 2.

Hand of Fulbert the Sinner.
Cambrai, Bibliothèque municipale, MS 864, fol. 23v (detail).
(By permission of the Bibliothèque municipale, Cambrai)

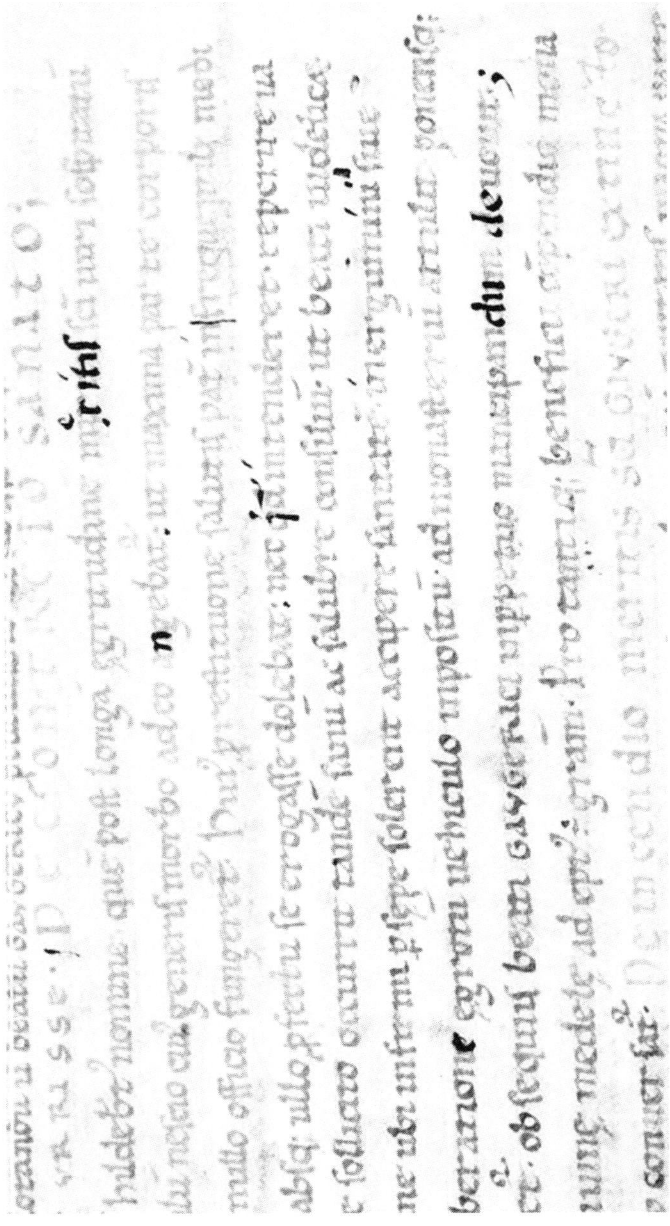

Figure 3.

Hand of Fulbert the Sinner.
Cambrai, Bibliothèque municipale, MS 864, fol. 125r (detail).
(By permission of the Bibliothèque municipale, Cambrai)

of their master. The first scribe takes over from Fulbert at folio 5r, line 18. He writes a very similar g, places r on the baseline, and makes similar wedges on his ascenders. However, he also places long s on the baseline, does not elongate x, and makes curly caudatae and angular ct-ligatures. Even more importantly, his writing is not as square as Fulbert's (fig. 4). This scribe wrote with a practiced hand that was struggling to imitate Fulbert's model. Other hands, however, are not as experienced and were struggling to get the words on the parchment, unable to emulate Fulbert's ductus and morphology.

Fulbert participated in all four codicological units that would eventually make up Cambrai 864. The manner of his participation is a clear sign of his authority within the scriptorium, and it indicates that even though he let his subordinates write long stints on their own, he was there to supervise and finish their work for them.

A remarkably large number of hands are interspersed with Fulbert's writing (table 1).[43] The Saint-Sépulcre obituary lists three scribes for this period—Lanvinus, Rodulfus, and Erlebodus—but in Cambrai 864 it appears that more than ten scribes cooperated, though it is difficult to distinguish between the various hands in this manuscript clearly. For a young monastery with a start-up scriptorium, this number is quite impressive. As a point of comparison: some fifteen scribes were active in the monastery of Michelsberg in Bamberg during the early twelfth century, out of the approximately seventy monks who inhabited that monastery.[44]

---

43. For similar cases, see Léon Gilissen, *L'expertise des écritures médiévales: Recherche d'une méthode avec application à un manuscrit du XIe siècle; Le lectionnaire de Lobbes, codex Bruxellensis 18018* (Ghent, 1973); and essays in *La collaboration*.

44. Karin Dengler-Schreiber, *Scriptorium und Bibliothek des Klosters Michelsberg in Bamberg* (Graz, 1979), 7–8, 75. The most prolific scribes here wrote about twenty books each, the "occasional" scribes about five; see Michael Gullick, "How Fast Did Scribes Write? Evidence from Ro-

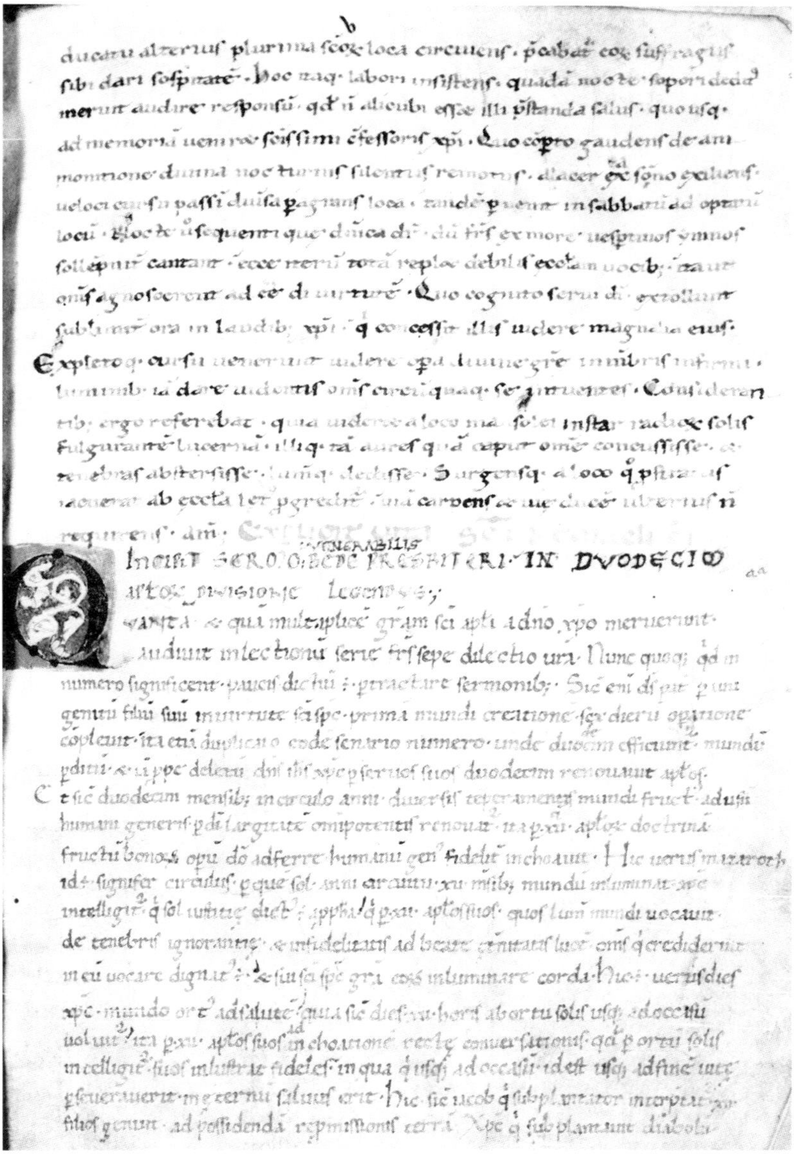

Figure 4.

Hand of Fulbert the Sinner (lns. 1–17) and another scribe (lns. 18–37).
Cambrai, Bibliothèque municipale, MS 864, fol. 5r.
(By permission of the Bibliothèque municipale, Cambrai)

Table 1.

Codicological Units and Scribes in
Cambrai, Bibliothèque municipale, MS 864.

Codicological Unit 1

    fols. 1r–5r   Fulbert the Sinner
    fols. 5r–23r   multiple hands (about 3)
    fols. 23v–25v   Fulbert the Sinner

Codicological Unit 2

    fols. 26r–124r   multiple hands (about 11)
    fols. 124v–125v   Fulbert the Sinner

Codicological Unit 3

    fols. 126r–149r   multiple hands (about 2)
    fols. 149r–149bisr   Fulbert the Sinner

Codicological Unit 4

    fols. 150r–176r   multiple hands (about 2)
    fols. 176v–208r   Fulbert the Sinner
    fols. 208v–214v   another hand (1 or more)
    fols. 215r–241r   Fulbert the Sinner
    fols. 241r–273v   multiple hands (about 5)

Behind the Scenes

If this ratio of scribes to monks is at all representative, more than ten professional scribes in Saint-Sépulcre would indicate a monastery of more than fifty monks. As many of the region's monasteries only housed between eight and eighteen monks in the late eleventh century, a complement of more than fifty monks would have turned Saint-Sépulcre into one of the most important and most commented-upon monasteries in the region.[45] This was clearly not the case. As we have seen, only "Abbot Walter and ten poor monks" inhabited the monastery in 1079, and nothing suggests that the monastery experienced sudden growth between 1080 and 1092. It is, therefore, unlikely that the hands in these codices all belonged to "professional," "full-time" scribes in the employ of Abbot Walter.

Two explanations for the abundance of hands in Cambrai 864 present themselves. The first is that scribes from Saint-Sépulcre only wrote a small part of the manuscript and that Fulbert used the services of several external scribes. He may have toured neighboring religious houses with the unfinished Cambrai 864, or he may have asked scribes from other monasteries or institutions to spend some time in Saint-Sépulcre to assist with manuscript production. However, the inexperience of many of the scribal hands argues against this hypothesis. From a "professional" scribe from the cathedral of Cambrai or one of Saint-Sépulcre's nearby

---

manesque Manuscripts," in *Making the Medieval Book: Techniques of Production. Proceedings of the Fourth Conference of the Seminar in the History of the Book to 1500, Oxford, July 1992,* ed. Linda L. Brownrigg (Los Altos, CA, 1995), 39–58 at 44.

45. An ideal number of monks was often thought to be around fifty, but numbers in this region were often down as low as twelve (Saint-Bertin in 1095–1123), eight to ten (Saint-Trond in the early twelfth century), and eighteen (Saint-Martin in Tournai in 1093). See Steven Vanderputten, "Monastic Recruitment in an Age of Reform (10th–12th Centuries): New Evidence for the Benedictine Abbey of Saint-Bertin," *Revue benedictine* 122 (2012): 232–51 at 244, 246.

abbeys such as Saint-Vaast or Saint-Amand, one expects reasonably regular and legible hands that are free from the typical errors made by scribes in training. However, Cambrai 864 is filled with irregularities, awkward decisions, and other evidence of general inexperience.

One of the most apparent signs of greenness in the manuscript is the irregularity of the ruling; the monks usually ruled manuscripts themselves and it did not require any particular talent to do so, just a bit of experience.[46] Armed with a dry point and a ruler, the individual who prepared the parchment had to exert light pressure on his pen to press about thirty parallel lines into a piece of parchment, which could then be used to write upon. The evenness of the distance between the lines was key. However, in Cambrai 864 the lines are sometimes crooked, and the distance between them is far from even (fig. 5). On folios 23r and 258r, for example, the smallest distance between two ruling lines measures 5.6 mm. and the largest 9.8 mm., which is a 77% difference. Around folio 100, the person who was ruling the parchment exercised so much force on his dry point that he repeatedly cut right through the parchment.

The second sign of general inexperience is the tendency to misjudge the amount of space that would be required to transcribe a text, even though (as we shall see) the scribes worked from excellent exemplars. Many scribes either left insufficient space at the start of a text for the rubricator to insert the title or else greatly overestimated the amount

---

46. Monasteries regularly started to buy fully prepared quires from commercial merchants only in the twelfth century (Gullick, "How Fast did Scribes Write?," 40). Thus, the Saint-Sépulcre scribes would likely have ruled their own manuscripts; compare Gullick, "How Fast did Scribes Write?," 54n12, and Richard Gameson, "A Scribe's Confession and the Making of the Anchin Hrabanus (Douai, Bibliothèque Municipale, Ms. 340)," in *Manuscripts in Transition: Recycling Manuscripts, Text and Images; Proceedings of the International Congress Held in Brussels (5–9 November 2002)*, ed. Brigitte Dekeyzer and Jan Van der Stock (Paris, 2005), 65–79.

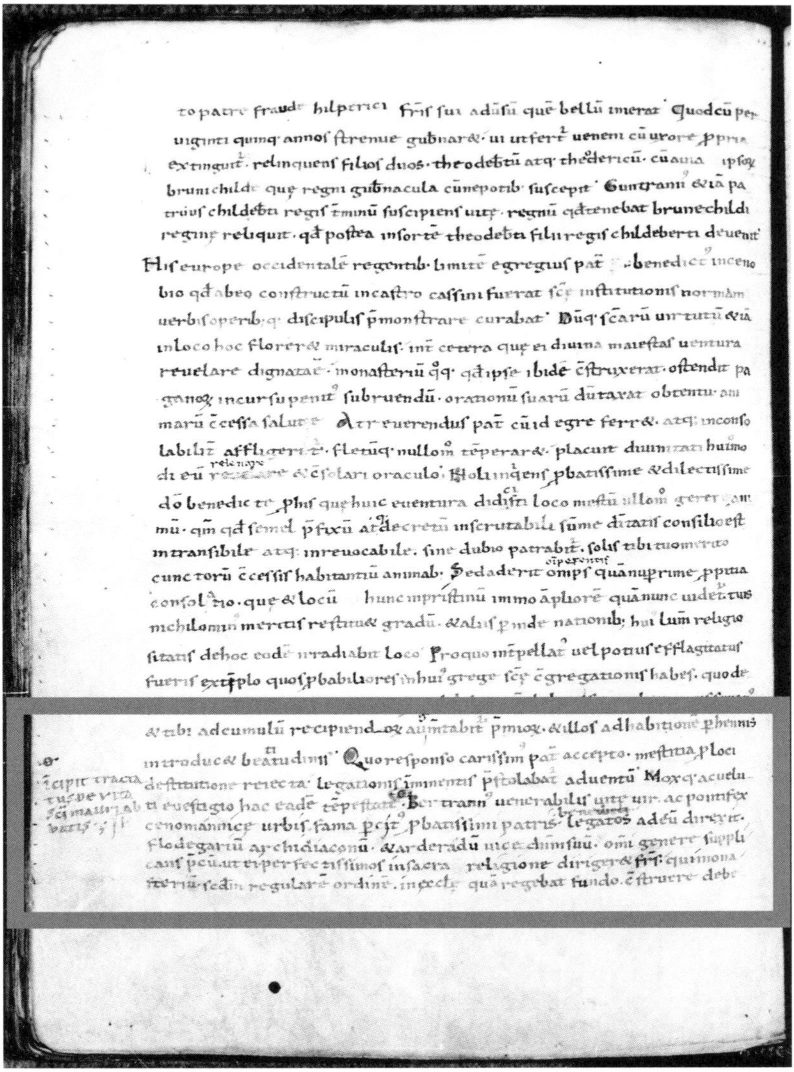

Figure 5.

Example of inexpert ruling and writing.
Cambrai, Bibliothèque municipale, 864, fol. 257v.
(By permission of the Bibliothèque municipale, Cambrai)

of space that would be needed (e.g., fols. 6r, 23v, 25r, 92r, 100v, 110r, 123v, 126r, 188r, 198v, and 272r). On five occasions, there was not enough room for a text to fit allotted, so the scribes had to reduce the size of the script and squeeze the last lines onto the margins (e.g., fols. 5v, 49v, 124v–125v, 202v–204r, and 241v–242r).

The third indication of lack of experience is manifest in the failure to coordinate a consistent layout. The fourth codicological unit of Cambria 864 starts with twenty-one folios laid out in two columns, whereas the preceding three units were written in long lines. When the scribe realized his mistake, he switched to long lines right in the middle of the text (fols. 171v–172r). Two folios later, Fulbert himself took over and wrote a lengthy stint of thirty-two folios himself—perhaps in sheer exasperation with the performance of his charges.

The other three hagiographical manuscripts in which Fulbert the Sinner participated evince the same general pattern. In Cambrai 807 Fulbert shows his leadership by writing the opening and closing pages of the codex (fols. 1r–17v and 109r–111v), but in between is a multitude of anonymous and often irregular hands. Cambrai 846 is mainly written by Fulbert (fols. 51v–144v), with the first fifty-one folios written only by two other scribes. In Cambrai 863, which is the sister volume to Cambrai 864, Fulbert wrote fols. 2v–7v, 41v, 200rb–254r, and possibly 61r, 142r, and 173r. Irregular hands that were prone to mistakes wrote the other folios. Though the codicological structure of this manuscript makes it harder to determine exactly which corrections were added at what time, it is clear the scribes repeatedly forgot to copy paragraphs and squeezed them into the margins (e.g., fol. 219r) or added them on scrap fragments of parchment (e.g., fols. 27r, 91r, 168r, and 173r). They forgot to copy the explicit or the incipit of a text on two occasions (fols. 109r, 113r), and generally failed to agree on a common layout.

From this combination of elements, it seems impossible that a group of highly experienced scribes from other institutions was asked to collaborate on these manuscripts. A second explanation for the number of hands that can be discerned in Cambrai 864 presents itself, namely, that virtually all Saint-Sépulcre's monks who knew how to write (in the technical sense of the word) were asked to participate in the production of this manuscript.

TEACHING THE SCRIBES

Were all these people learning how to write in a "house style" under the guidance of Fulbert the Sinner? All the hands show a basic similarity, influenced at least by the fact that the scribes were all writing in the same environment, at the same time, and using the same exemplars, but they do not appear consciously to imitate Fulbert's hand. As can be seen in a comparison of Fulbert's formation of the letter **g** and **ex**-ligatures with those of other scribes (fig. 6 and compare to fig. 1), it is clear these scribes did not attempt to imitate the morphology or ductus of Fulbert's writing.[47] The descender of **g**, for example, is sometimes open and sometimes closed, and is usually attached to the right of the upper bowl and sometimes to the left, but never in the middle as was Fulbert's habit. Similar observations can be made for other letters and ligatures. Fulbert apparently placed no high value on stylistic homogeneity within the manuscripts produced under his guidance.

This lack of stylistic homogeneity also applies to the illumination and layout of these codices. The texts in Cambrai 846 were written in two columns of twenty-six lines, while the texts in other manuscripts were written in long lines from thirty-two (Cambrai 807) up to thirty-eight (Cambrai 863). The titles of saints' lives are sometimes executed as rubrics, in red undercast letters, and sometimes written in capitals in-filled with red, green, or yellow pigment. These

---

47. For similar cases, see Tibbets, "*Praescriptiones*," 32–34.

Figure 6.

Hands of Various Scribes in
Cambrai, Bibliothèque municipale, MS 864
Showing Formation of "g" and "ex."

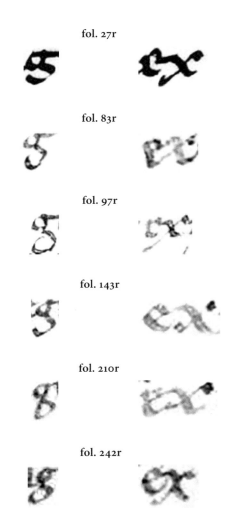

variations in layout have no specific significance. They do not change the meaning of the texts. They only indicate the lack of coordination between scribes. What these manuscripts do have in common, however, is that they were all executed in a simple layout that did not require the intervention of a trained illuminator. The initials are small and plain, colored in red with sometimes a dot of green or yellow, but with no decoration to speak of—the scribes themselves evidently did them. A small number of initials were illuminated more elaborately, though in a rather crude style. They may be later additions, or perhaps practice runs of an aspiring illuminator among the Saint-Sépulcre scribes.

Were the scribes forgoing to coordinate the style of their codices because they were in too much of a hurry? Probably not. They wrote their texts using the relay method, in which one scribe writes some lines, then stops (often at a seemingly random point), at which point another scribe takes over.[48] The scribes alternated frequently and often wrote but very short fragments of text. The following example from Cambrai 864 (figs. 7–8) demonstrates the frequency of these changes: two hands wrote folio 81v (A, lns. 1–9; and B, lns. 10–36); at the top of folio 82r hand A began again (lns. 1–18), was interrupted by B (lns. 19–24), who was corrected by a later hand X; and hand A took over again and finished the folio (lns. 25–36).

This writing method did not facilitate or expedite the production process, because the scribes had to wait for one another to finish before they could start writing their lines, instead of being able to work simultaneously. The hands keep alternating throughout the codex—sometimes writing thirty folios, sometimes just a couple of lines. The most regular hands tend to write longer fragments of texts, whereas the untrained hands only write a few lines. The fairly irreg-

---

48. Benjamin Victor, "Simultaneous Copying of Classical Texts 800–1100: Techniques and Their Consequences," in *La collaboration*, 325–45.

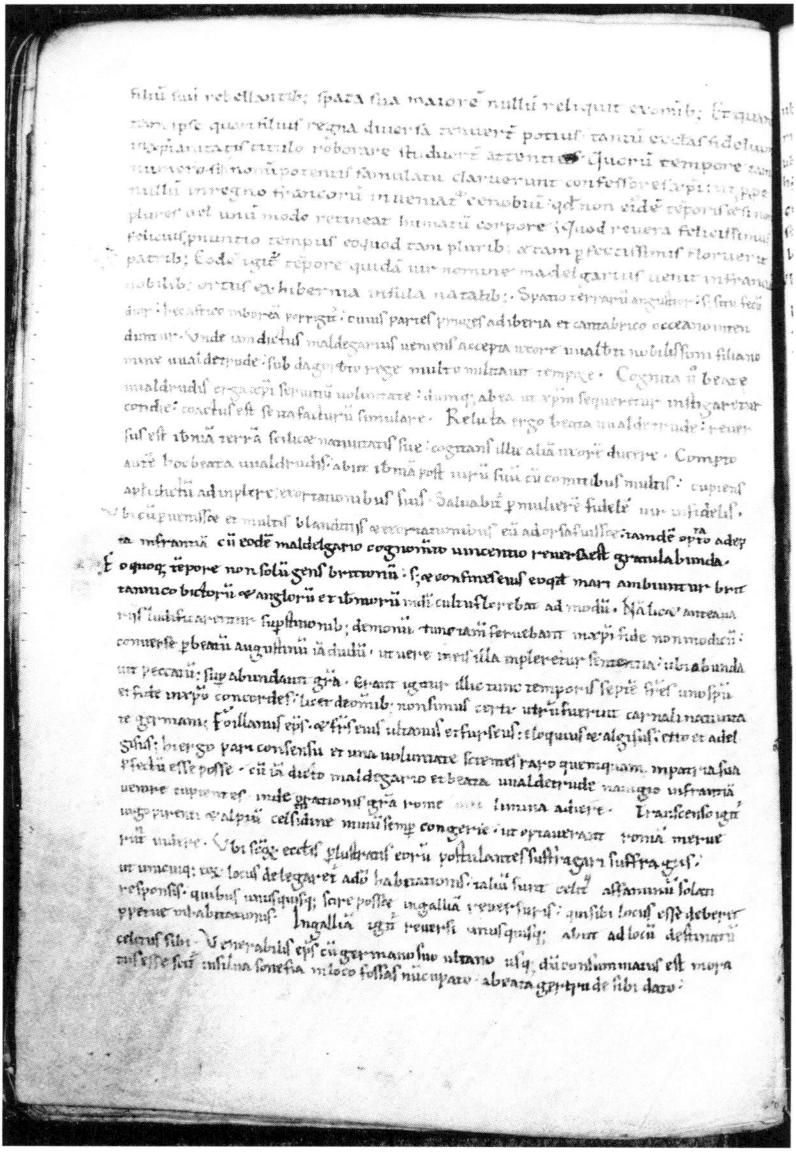

Figure 7.

Hands A (lns. 1–9) and B (lns. 10–36).
Cambrai, Bibliothèque municipale, 864, fol. 81v.
(By permission of the Bibliothèque municipale, Cambrai)

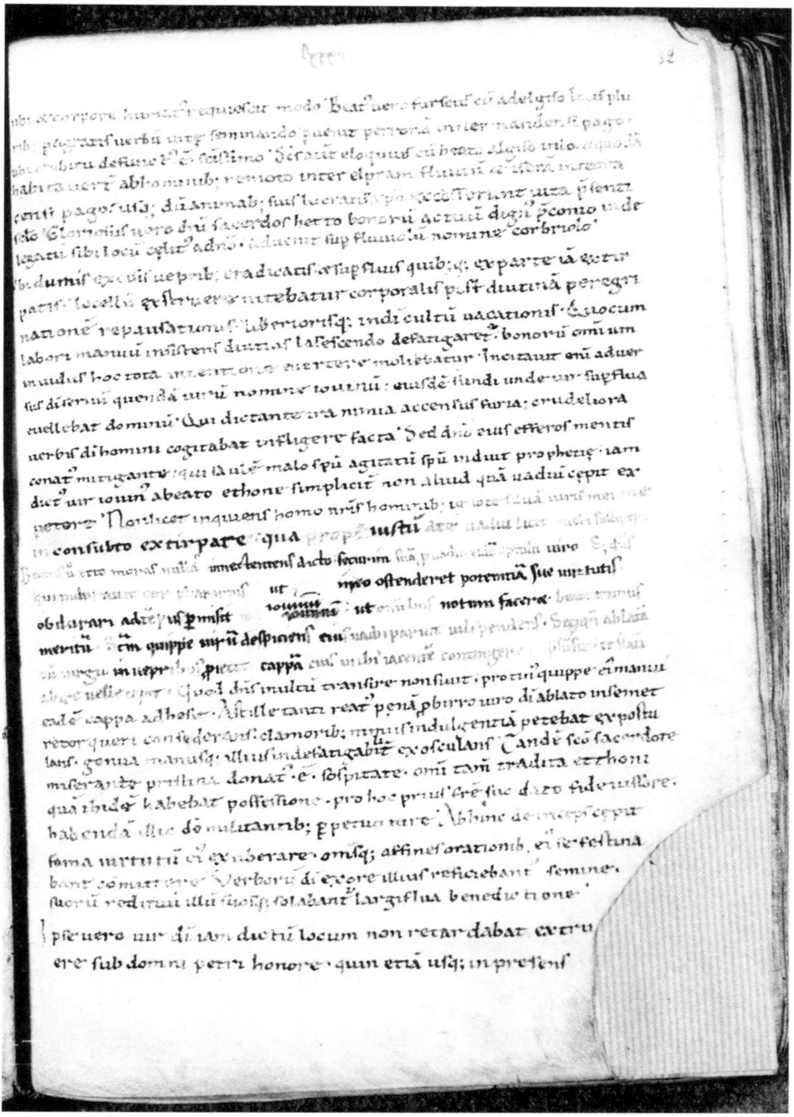

Figure 8.

Hands A (lns. 1–18 and 25–36) and B (lns. 19–24).
Cambrai, Bibliothèque municipale, 864, fol. 82r.
(By permission of the Bibliothèque municipale, Cambrai)

ular hand B, for example, contributed only four short pieces and wrote no more than one folio in total—as if his participation in the codex were tolerated rather than encouraged.

While Fulbert the Sinner single-handedly copied hundreds of folios with important spiritual texts, he could not fill Saint-Sépulcre's entire library by himself. He conceivably requested the participation of his colleagues, even if they were unqualified, for the less critical manuscripts. Those who were able to hold a pen may have dashed off to the scriptorium in between the liturgical hours to do their bit. This working method would explain the inexperienced hands, the short writing stints, and the frequent changes of ink in the midst of a folio.

The most inexperienced hands are concentrated in the second codicological unit of Cambrai 864 (fols. 26r–125v). Fulbert had acquired an excellent exemplar for these folios, one that was fit to be copied with only minimal changes, so that the copying process of fols. 26–125 should have been straightforward enough for beginners. This exemplar (Cambrai, Bibliothèque municipale, MS 865) was produced shortly after 1051 in the Cathedral of Cambrai.[49] The Cathedral and Saint-Sépulcre were situated at walking distance from one another in the city of Cambrai and both owed loyalty to the bishop. As a result, the two institutions maintained very close contact during the last quarter of the eleventh century, and the canons apparently lent Cambrai 865 to their neighbors.[50] This manuscript consisted of three codicological units. The first (fols. 1r–71r), which was produced in the first half of the eleventh century and was probably not, in fact, produced in the Cathedral of Cambrai, concentrated fully on Saint Rémi, the archbishop of Reims, and was copied integrally into Cambrai 864. The second unit (fols. 72r–75r) is a later addition of two bifolia with the life

---

49. See Muzerelle, *Manuscrits datés ... Cambrai*, 103.
50. Ibid., xxiii.

Behind the Scenes

of Giles of Athens.[51] And the third unit (fols. 76r–171r) contains a Life of Saint Géry, dedicated to Bishop Gerard I of Cambrai (1012–51), as well as a selection of fourteen saints' lives, seven of which were copied into the manuscript from Saint-Sépulcre.

The scribes of Saint-Sépulcre copied most of the saints from the exemplar in their original sequence, as can be seen in table 2. Around the end of the eleventh century, it was still somewhat unusual to copy a hagiographical exemplar so fully. Scribes in this area would typically compile hagiographical manuscripts from a large number of exemplars, copying only those texts that held a particular interest for their specific community.[52] The idea of a fixed list of saints (other than the apostles) who were important to all communities only started to gain ground in the second half of the twelfth century, and would become truly popular with Jacob de Voragine's *Golden Legend* (ca. 1265). Around the end of the eleventh century, the relatively slavish copying of a collection of saints' lives was a sign of extreme reverence for the exemplar, or similarly special circumstances.

The Saint-Sépulcre scribes copied each text in their exemplar as faithfully as possible. A critical edition of the *Vita tertia Gaugerici* in Cambrai 865 and Cambrai 864 by Steven Vanderputten and Diane Reilly shows a negligible

---

51. *BHL*, 107, nos. 93–94.
52. Diane J. Reilly, "The Cluniac Giant Bible and the *Ordo librorum ad legendum*: A Reassessment of Monastic Bible Reading and Cluniac Customary Instructions," in *From Dead of Night to End of Day: The Medieval Customs of Cluny*, ed. Susan Boynton and Isabelle Cochelin (Turnhout, 2005), 177–78, 182–83; Tjamke Snijders, *Manuscript Communications: Visual and Textual Mechanics of Communication in Hagiographic Manuscripts from the Southern Low Countries* (Turnhout, 2015), 148–75, 323–31. In 1131 Saint-Sépulcre possessed twenty-eight relics from the Cambrai area, including those of "Sanctus Gaugericus episcopus et confessor ab urbe Cameracensi," "Sanctus Etto confessor a [villa Dompierre]," and "Sanctus Vincentius confessor a vico Sonegias"; see Rodulf of Saint-Sépulcre, "Vita Lietberti," 868.

Table 2.

Contents of Cambrai, Bibliothèque municipale, MSS 865 and 864.

Cambrai 865 (Exemplar: Cambrai Cathedral)		Cambrai 864 (Copy: Saint-Sépulcre)	
Remigius of Reims	*10 January*	*Remigius of Reims*	*10 January*
Giles of Athens/Septimania	*(later add.)*	*Holy Cross*	*(1 fol., later add.?)*
Vincentius Madelgarius of Soignies	*14 July*	*Remigius of Reims, cont.*	*10 January*
Evurtius of Orléans	*9 July*	*Etto of Flanders*	*10 July*
Etto of Flanders	*10 July*	*Evurtius of Orléans*	*9 July*
Maximinus of Trèves	*29 May*		
Marculfus of Nanteuil	*1 May*		
Hilarius of Arle	*5 May*		
Albinus of Angers	*1 March*		
Brigida of Kildaria	*1 February*		
Amandus of Tongeren/Maastricht	*6 February*	*Amandus of Tongeren/Maastricht*	*6 February*
Ambrosius of Milan	*14 June*	*Ambrosius of Milan*	*14 June*
Furseus of Lagny	*16 January*	*Furseus of Lagny*	*16 January*
Gregorius of Langres	*4 January*	*Gregorius of Langres*	*4 January*
Gaugericus of Cambrai	*11 August*	*Gaugericus of Cambrai*	*11 August*

Behind the Scenes

amount of textual variants between the two manuscripts.[53] While the Saint-Sépulcre scribes did not copy the lives of seven saints in Cambrai 865 that apparently did not interest them—some because they may have been too foreign, others because they already possessed a copy of their life—they did not consciously try to rewrite the texts or otherwise improve on their exemplar.[54] The only scribe in Saint-Sépulcre who played with the text in Cambrai 865 and strove to improve it was Fulbert the Sinner. When his fellow monks had faithfully copied the *Vita tertia Gaugerici* with one folio to spare, he used that folio to squeeze in four new miracles of Gaugericus, which he probably authored himself.[55]

Cambrai 865 was an easy exemplar to work with because it was neatly written and its layout was clear and not unlike that of Cambrai 864. In other words, it must have been relatively easy to copy this manuscript, even for an inexperienced scribe. The monks from Saint-Sépulcre who worked on the second codicological unit thus did not need to be creative or to make hard decisions, but only had to reproduce the text and layout of the exemplar before them.

The *Vita sancti Humberti*, elsewhere in the manuscript, shows the risk of giving these inexperienced scribes less-than-perfect exemplars. Humbertus was the founder of the Abbey of Maroilles at some twenty-five miles from the city

---

53. Gerard of Cambrai, *Acta Synodi Atrebatensis, Vita Autberti, Vita tertia Gaugerici, Varia scripta ex officina Gerardi exstantia*, ed. Steven Vanderputten and Diane Reilly, Corpus Christianorum, Continuatio medievalis 270 (Turnhout, 2014), 141.

54. When Bishop Lietbertus founded Saint-Sépulcre in 1064, he donated a relic of Vincentius Madelgarius of Soignies. This saint's Life was not copied into Cambrai 864, but that can hardly be because the monks were not interested in him. In all probability, they already possessed a Life of this saint. See Rodulf of Saint-Sépulcre, "Vita Lietberti," 868.

55. *Acta Synodi Atrebatensis*, 141–42.

of Cambrai.[56] His *Vita* was an important text for the community of Saint-Sépulcre because Bishop Lietbertus had donated one of Humbertus's relics to them.[57] One of the Saint-Sépulcre scribes began to copy Humbertus's *Vita prima*,[58] but neglected to read through the entire text of his exemplar before he started his copying work. He copied down how Humbertus was born in the time of Childeric II and lived an exemplary life in the Church.[59] One day, Humbertus decided to visit his parents' possessions in Rome, traveling with Saints Amandus and Nicasius. When a bear killed one of the saints' packhorses, Humbertus made the beast carry their luggage. After his sojourn in Rome, Humbertus returned home, but he pined for the papal city and made another pilgrimage. The pope then ordered him to go back and construct a church.

At this moment in the story, the scribe's working method caused a severe difficulty. When he was about to start copying folio 141r, he learned that Humbertus indeed returned home and received permission from the bishop of Cambrai to found a monastery on his land of Maricolas (Maroilles), whereupon twelve monks came to live there. However, Humbertus soon realized that his monks would not prevail on the path of the Rule of Benedict ("Videns autem postea quia monachorum congregatio ibidem juxta tramitem regulae sancti Benedicti non valeret esse"). He, therefore, decided to abandon his monastery and instead construct a far

---

56. Anne-Marie Helvétius, "Réécriture hagiographique et réforme monastique: Les premières *Vitae* de Saint Humbert de Maroilles (Xe–XIe siècles), avec l'édition de la *Vita Humberti Prima*," in *La réécriture hagiographique dans l'Occident médiéval: Transformations formelles et idéologiques,* ed. Monique Goullet and Martin Heinzelmann (Ostfildern, 2003), 195–230.

57. Rodulf of Saint-Sépulcre, "Vita Lietberti," 868.

58. *BHL*, 601, nos. 4037–38.

59. Cambrai 864, fol. 139v. The scribe copied chapters 2–7; see Helvétius, "Réécriture hagiographique," 221–24.

Behind the Scenes

more popular house for canons in the vicinity. The rest of the *Vita prima* deals with Humbertus's life as the head of this chapter.

Imagine our scribe's surprise. This *Vita prima* was not a story that celebrated the life of Humbertus as the abbot of Maroilles, and would not exactly inspire the monks of newly-founded Saint-Sépulcre. He immediately stopped his copying work, and presumably did some further research (or asked Fulbert the Sinner for help). He soon discovered that between 1030 and 1035 a *Vita secunda Humberti* had been composed in which Humbertus did found the monastery of Maroilles, embrace the Rule of Benedict, and remain Maroilles's abbot until his death around 680.

An experienced scribe could have solved this problem without too much difficulty, combining the beginning of the *Vita prima* with the ending of the *Vita secunda*—a challenging task, but not an insurmountable one. Alternatively, he could have cut folio 140r–v from the codex, scraped the text on folio 139v, and created a palimpsest, thus replacing the *Vita prima* with the *Vita secunda*. However, being inexperienced, this scribe simply crossed out the part of the *Vita prima* he already wrote, tried to scrape the text from the first folio but failed to do so in a way that would permit him to create a palimpsest, and quickly abandoned his attempts (fig. 9). He just continued on folio 141v with the *Vita secunda* as if nothing had happened, using a different pen and ink (fig. 10).

The scribes of Cambrai 864 were clearly given a measure of individual responsibility to pick and choose their texts. If an experienced scribe such as Fulbert had been intimately involved in matters of text choice, obvious mistakes as with the *Vita prima Humberti* would either not have been made at all, or would have been solved more professionally. Fulbert was either too busy to supervise these monks as closely as he should have, or he consciously let his subordinates make their own mistakes, perhaps judging that in this par-

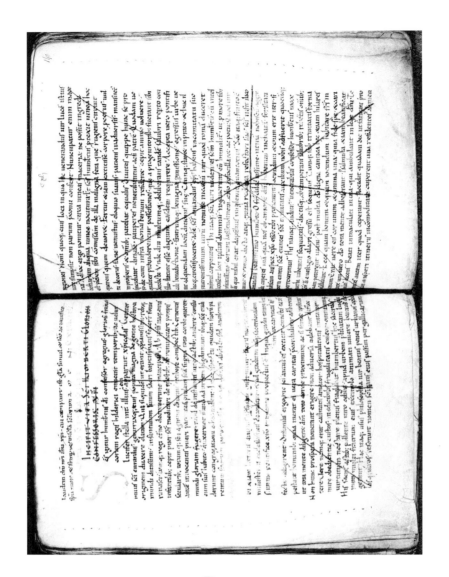

Figure 9.

Opening of the *Vita prima Humberti*.
Cambrai, Bibliothèque municipale, 864, fols. 139v–140r.
(By permission of the Bibliothèque municipale, Cambrai)

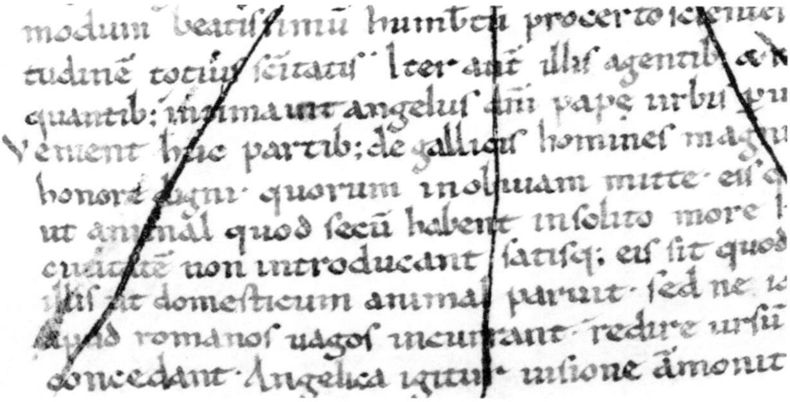

Figure 10a.

Hand of the *Vita prima Humberti*.
Cambrai, Bibliothèque municipale, 864, fol. 141v (detail).
(By permission of the Bibliothèque municipale, Cambrai)

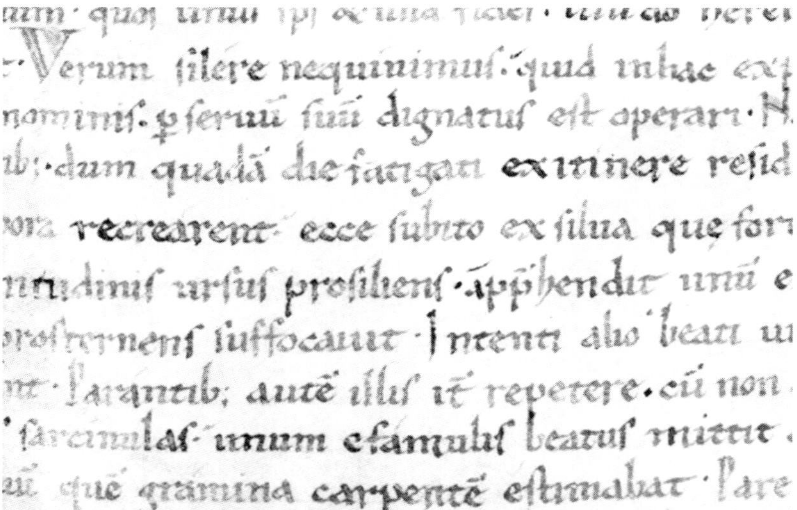

Figure 10b.

Hand of the *Vita secunda Humberti*.
Cambrai, Bibliothèque municipale, 864, fol. 143r (detail).
(By permission of the Bibliothèque municipale, Cambrai)

ticular case, their participation in the process of creation was more important than the aesthetics of the end result.

This last point deserves some further investigation. Was there some sort of spiritual value to writing Cambrai 864 as a team effort? On the surface, the situation is reminiscent of Richard Gameson's study of a manuscript with canon law from the nearby monastery of Saint-Vaast that was produced by nine scribes in twelve stints. These scribes all signed their work and asked for the monastery's patron saint to accept their work and look after them.[60] Gameson classified this manuscript as "an exercise in recording and apotheosing the scriptorium itself." However, in the case of Saint-Sépulcre, it was not a small team of well-trained scribes but a less experienced group of monks who produced the codex—and instead of writing a high-status, luxury manuscript with canon law that was meant for an expert audience, they worked on a middle range hagiographical codex.

The choice of genre is meaningful, as hagiography was among the few genres in an eleventh-century monastery that did not need to be copied perfectly and flawlessly. In copying the Bible, the sacred nature of the text prohibited conscious alteration, just as the respect in which the Church Fathers were traditionally held inhibited changes to their works. Saints' lives, on the other hand, allowed a scribe a certain freedom for improvisation and error without immediate repercussions, as long as the scribe respected the spiritual truth of the narrative.[61] From a spiritual point of view, it mattered little whether Humbertus had blue or grey eyes, whether he led a house for canons or a monastery, or

---

60. Arras, Bibliothèque municipale, MS 723; Gameson, "'Signed' Manuscripts," 53–57.

61. See Monique Goullet, *Écriture et réécriture hagiographiques: Essai sur les réécritures de vies de saints dans l'Occident latin médiéval (VIIIe–XIIIe s.)* (Turnhout, 2005); and Goullet and Heinzelmann, *La réécriture hagiographique*.

how exactly he tamed the bear that killed his horse, as long as his sanctity shone through every description and his every deed.[62] The purpose of a hagiographical narrative was to convey the idea of the saint's sanctity to an audience, rather than inform them about the biographical particulars of his earthly existence. As a result, scribes had always been free to play with hagiographical texts, update them to the requirements of their environments, commit mistakes, and learn how to correct them in a way that was not possible in many other genres. Hagiography was, in other words, a perfect teaching genre.

Secondly, hagiography was easy to read and understand. Contemporaries often repeated that saints' lives were suitable for people who were taking their very first steps on the path of Christian devotion, as the simple stories about saints and their adventures could inspire even the most uncultured monk.[63] All the monks in Saint-Sépulcre, even the least educated, could thus have worked on this hagiographical codex while understanding what they were writing.

Finally, hagiography was read aloud in front of the entire community during Matins and meal breaks. The large audience gave a hagiographical codex the power to communicate ideas and ideologies to all monks, thereby strengthening their sense of community. In essence, hagiography was aimed at the community rather than the individual.[64] Contrary to the Saint-Vaast example, the manuscript

---

62. "Georgii Florentii Gregorii episcopi Turonensis libri octo Miraculorum," in *Gregorii episcopi Turonensis Miracula et opera minora*, ed. Bruno Krusch, Monumenta Germaniae historica, Scriptores rerum merovingicarum 1.2 (Hannover, 1885; nov. ed. 1969), 1–370 at 212.

63. William of St.-Thierry, *Un traité de la vie solitaire: Epistola ad fratres de Monte-Dei de Guillaume de Saint-Thierry; Édition critique du texte latin,* ed. Marie-Madeleine Davy, 2 vols. (Paris, 1940), 1:81, 120–21.

64. Ineke van 't Spijker, "Model Reading: Saints' Lives and Literature of Religious Formation in the Eleventh and Twelfth Centuries," in *"Scribere sanctorum gesta": Recueil d'études d'hagiographie médiévale offert à Guy*

from Saint-Sépulcre was created by a large part of the monastic community—possibly even the entire community—for the entire community. It was a deliberately simple exercise in which all monks could participate and taste the satisfaction of producing a manuscript together and then listen to their work being read aloud to everyone. The various monks participated at their level of competence. Some were struggling to write at all. Others may have been trying their hands at the selection of texts, whereas the most experienced hands attempted to imitate Fulbert's *praescriptio*. As such, each monk of Saint-Sépulcre participated according to his ability.

CONCLUSION

When Fulbert the Sinner transferred from Normandy to the monastery of Saint-Sépulcre in Cambrai, he arrived in a small, struggling start-up without the means to invest in a scriptorium. Nevertheless, the community needed manuscripts, so Fulbert set to work. The thirteen preserved manuscripts indicate that he wrote more than 1,100 folios of foundational texts: *The Monk's Diadem,* Cassian's *Institutiones* and *Conferences,* Gregory the Great's *Commentary in Job.* As he could not fill the entire library himself, he enlisted his fellow monks.

Fulbert's habit of signing his manuscripts grants us an unusual glimpse into the organization of this young and relatively insignificant scriptorium. Fulbert was clearly the scribe in charge, who reserved essential texts for himself while leaving the hagiographical codices to others. Some of these other scribes had trained hands, but most were struggling. Fulbert borrowed at least one good hagiographical exemplar from the Cathedral of Cambrai to make the work

---

Phillipart, ed. Étienne Rénard et al., Hagiologia 3 (Turnhout, 2005), 135–56 at 144–50.

easier for them. However, he did not ostensibly train the Saint-Sépulcre monks to achieve a recognizable style, with a fixed ductus and a clear layout. Instead, he appears to have allowed these monks to write largely unsupervised, at least when it came to hagiography. The hagiographical codices were suitable for beginners because they were important to the community without containing incomprehensibly abstract reasoning or requiring the scribes to copy their exemplars perfectly.

Fulbert's decision to enlist the monks of Saint-Sépulcre as scribes ensured the rapid and cost-effective creation of the hagiographical codices that were required for the liturgy. His decision had spiritual benefits as well. In the monastic context, writing was seen as a spiritually beneficial act in and of itself: it was entirely equivalent to work or prayer.[65] As such, the monks' work was not just a pragmatic way of producing more manuscripts: it was a shared spiritual exercise, the fruit of which was read to the entire community during Matins and mealtimes. When the monks were sitting together to listen in reverent silence to the result of their handiwork, the manuscript was more than just the sum of its texts: it was an object that stood for teamwork, unity of purpose, and communality. Cambrai 864 enacted the fellowship of the Saint-Sépulcre monks through a multiplicity of hands and texts. As such, the manuscript was the material apotheosis of this newly founded monastery.

KU Leuven

---

65. Scribe Rudolph of Saint-Vaast remarks in the eleventh century that every letter, ruled line, and pricking hole that he executed represents a forgiven sin: Arras, Bibliothèque municipale, MS 860, fol. 1r (for a transcription, see Gameson, "'Signed' Manuscripts," 72). This sentiment is echoed by many, among whom Orderic Vitalis remarked in the early twelfth-century that every letter of "a huge volume of the divine law" (*divinae legis*) was weighed against the sins of the scribe: Orderic Vitalis, *The Ecclesiastical History of Orderic Vitalis*, ed. and trans. Marjorie Chibnall, 6 vols. (Oxford, 1969–80), 2:50.

Index of Manuscripts Cited

Arras
Bibliothèque municipale
MS 14: 115n32
MS 573: 115n32
MS 723: 142n60
MS 860: 145n65
MS 1029: 13n22, 115n32

Athens
National Bank of Greece Cultural Foundation
MS Pezarou 50: 78n35

Avranches
Bibliothèque municipale
MS 99: 13n22

Besançon
Bibliothèque municipale
MS 33: 78n35

Boulogne-sur-mer
Bibliothèque municipale
MS 106: 113n22

Brussels
KBR
MS II 992: 113n22, 115n32
MS 14682: 115n32

Cambrai
Bibliothèque municipale = Médiathèque d'agglomération
MS 215: 109n11, 116n38, 117
MS 216: 110n12, 116n38
MS 217: 109n11, 116n38
MS 218: 109n11, 116n38

Index of Manuscripts

MS 219: 110n12, 116n38
MS 247: 109n11, 116n37
MS 504: 110n12, 116n37
MS 506: 110n12
MS 544: 111n18
MS 807: 110n12, 117, 117n40, 128–29
MS 819: 109n11, 116n36
MS 846: 110n12, ,117n40
MS 863: 110n12, 117, 117n40, 128–29
MS 864: 110, 110n12, 111–12, 113n23, 115n32, 117, 117n40, 118, *119, 120, 121,* 122, *123, 124,* 125–26, *127,* 128–29, *130,* 131, *132, 133,* 134–35, *136,* 137–38, 138n59, 139, *140, 141*
MS 865: 134–35, *136,* 137

Douai
Bibliothèque Marceline Desbordes-Valmore
MS 68: 115n32
MS 151: 115n32
MS 836: 111n18, 115n32
MS 867: 111n18, 113n23, 115n32
MS 899: 107n4

Edinburgh
National Library of Scotland
Advocates MS 72.1.4: 69

Florence
Biblioteca Medicea Laurenziana
MS Conv. soppr. 35: 78n35
MS Conv. soppr. 36: 78n35, 101
MS Plut. 7.10: 86, 86n55, 88n57
MS Plut. 32.9: 86n55
MS Plut. 40.7: 1, 4, 4n9, 5, 29, 29n24, 30–31, *33,* 34, 34n28, 36–37, *38, 39,* 40, 42, *44,* 46, *47,* 50–51, *52,* 54, *55,* 56–57, 57n50, *58,* 59, *60,* 61
MS Strozzi 152: 2, 2nn3–4

Lille
Archives départmentales du Nord
3H2/5: 107n3

3H56: 107n3
3H73: 107n3
3H255: 107n3
3H256: 107n3
3H257: 107n3

London
  British Library
    Add. MS 19352: 94
    Add. MS 19587: 2, 2nn3–4
    Add. MS 36928: 72, 72nn22–23, 74
    Add. MS 40731: 78n35
    Add. MS 40753: 78n35
    Harley MS 5537: 70, 70n18
    Royal MS 2.A.vi: 78n35
  Victoria and Albert Museum
    MS L.475-1918: 3, 3n7

Milan
  Biblioteca Ambrosiana
    MS B 1 sup.: 78n35
  Biblioteca Trivulziana
    MS 340: 788n35

Mt. Athos
  Dionysiou Monastery
    MS 65: 96, 97, 101
    MS 565: 78n35
    MS 585: 78n35
  Great Lavra Monastery
    MS B 12: 78n35
  Kausokalybion Monastery
    MS 87: 78n35
  Vatopedi Monastery
    MS 1231: 78n35

Mt. Sinai
  Monastery of Saint Catherine
    MS gr. 64: 78n35
    MS gr. 65: 78n35, 101

Index of Manuscripts

  MS gr. 1275: 96n80
  MS gr. 2054: 78n35

Munich
 Bayerische Staatsbibliothek
  Cgm 8950: 69

New York
 Morgan Library and Museum
  MS M.676: 61n56

Oxford
 Bodleian Library
  MS Bodley 852 (2611): 112, 113n23
  MS Canon. gr. 114: 78n35
  MS E. D. Clarke 15: 63, 65–66, 67, 68–70, 71, 72, 72n23, 73, 74, 75, 80, 80nn38–39, 81–100, 101n92, 103–4
  MS Wake 44: 78n35

Paris
 Bibliothèque nationale de France
  MS gr. 164: 101n90
  MS italien 74: 3
  MS lat. 1805: 113n22
  MS NAF 4119: 1, 4, 4n9, 5, 5n11, 6, 6n14, 7, 7n15, 14, 15, 17, 19, 21n20, 22, 23, 25, 26, 28–29
  MS NAF 4530: 1, 4, 4n9, 5, 5n11, 6–7, 7n15, 11, 12, 13, 37
  MS Par. gr. 41: 78n35

Rouen
 Bibliothèque municipale
  MS 1405 (Y.27): 114n28
  MS 1409 (Y.189): 112, 113n23

St. Petersburg
 Russian National Library
  MS gr. 348: 78n35

Valenciennes
　Bibliothèque municipale
　　MS 514: 111n18, 115n32

Vatican City
　Biblioteca Apostolica Vaticana
　　MS Vat. gr. 342: 72, 72nn21–23
　　MS Vat. gr. 752: 77n33

Venice
　Bibliotheca Nazionale Marciana
　　MS gr. 17: 77

Vienna
　Österreichische Nationalbibliothek
　　MS suppl. gr 47: 64
　　MS theol. gr. 8: 77n33
　　MS theol. gr. 336: 102

SAINT LOUIS UNIVERSITY VATICAN FILM LIBRARY MELLON FELLOWSHIPS

Short-term fellowships of between two and eight weeks are available for research in the collections of the Vatican Film Library at Saint Louis University. The subject of study may be in an area, but must be supported by the Vatican Film Library's collections of microfilmed medieval and Renaissance manuscripts from the Biblioteca Apostolica Vaticana and other libraries or of microfilmed Jesuit historical documents. Applicants must possess an earned doctorate or be a PhD candidate at the dissertation stage. The fellowship provides a stipend of $2,250 per month and travel within the continental United States.

http://lib.slu.edu/special-collections/research/fellowship

SAINT LOUIS UNIVERSITY CENTER FOR MEDIEVAL & RENAISSANCE STUDIES NEH RESEARCH FELLOWSHIPS

Short-term fellowships of five, ten, or fifteen weeks are available for research in the collections of the Vatican Film Library, as well as the manuscript, rare books, and general collections of Pius XII Memorial Library at Saint Louis University. Topics proposed for research may include any medieval or early modern subject. Applicants must possess an earned doctorate or be a PhD candidate at the dissertation stage. The fellowship provides a stipend of $1,750 per five-week period, travel expenses, and a furnished apartment. Fellows are required to give one public lecture on the topic of their research.

http://www.slu.edu/arts-and-sciences/medieval-renaissance-studies/fellowships.php